Lost In The Woods

A 12 Step Approach
To Spiritual Growth

Douglas Gast

Fairway Press
Lima, Ohio

LOST IN THE WOODS

Library of Congress Catalog Card Number: 93-74994

7998 / ISBN 1-55673-827-7
PRINTED IN U.S.A.

To my:

Parents who loved me and believed in me even when I couldn't do either myself

Wonderful wife who has been a source of continual support, love and encouragement in this and every adventure of our life together

Four Great children who keep me humble, young at heart, proud to be called dad and always looking for joy and excitement in life

Secretary Maria who very patiently and graciously deciphered and decoded the original draft of the text. Truly a God-send.

Second family at St. Philip who in our 10 years of partnership in ministry taught me what it really means to be the Family of God and how strongly God's Spirit could move in a congregation

Friends in AA, especially all the members of the groups that met at St. Philip. Your kindnesses and sharing touch my heart and life. Thank God for allowing our lives to meet.

Advisor and mentor Paul Swanson. His gifts in counseling and insights in faith and people have always influenced me

Good Friend Shirley whose words of encourgement and expressions of support were the real catalyst getting this manuscript published.

To each of these very special people and many more, especially to my personal Higher Power Jesus Christ, I owe a debt of eternal thanks.

Table Of Contents

Chapter 1

Beginning The Spiritual Journey

A long time ago in a mystical kingdom far away on a bright and beautiful day, a man decided to take a walk in the nearby forest. At first the walk was invigorating. He beheld the wonders of the forest. But as time passed he began to realize that he was lost. For hours he searched to find a way out but to no avail. Then as the shadows lengthened and darkness took hold, the man began to lament over his lostness. If only he would have stayed in the safety of his own home. If only he had not gone into the forest in the first place. If only he had paid more attention to the landmarks along the way. If only he had not ventured so far into the forest. But it was too late for that now. He was alone, saddened, discouraged, and fearful of ever finding a way out again. But then, all of a sudden, he heard what sounded like someone walking not far from where he was sitting. He jumped up and ran to where he had heard the noise coming from. Sure enough, there was another man walking through the forest. "Stop, friend, stop," the first man called out. "Am I glad to see you. You see I've been in these woods all day and apparently I've gotten turned around, lost my bearing, and can no longer find a way out. Dear friend, please, will you show me the way? I am too frightened and too lost to ever make my way out alone." "No, I don't mind you joining me," said the second man. "The company would be good to have, for I too am scared and all alone. But before we go one step farther, I must tell you that I too am lost and there is no way that I can show anyone the way out. But I do have an idea. Let's sit down here now, figure out what we've done, where we've been, what we have tried that doesn't work, and maybe we can figure out something together that might work."

That story comes from a friend in AA. He would often tell it as an opening story as a preface to what he would be sharing as a speaker to his audience. It was his way of introducing himself and the description of his spiritual journey. It is an apt description of my spiritual journey as well. People identify with that story because it touches their own experience of lostness and their search to find a way out. They are searching for meaning and purpose in their lives and living. The pursuit to find a way out has taken a myriad of forms and expressions. Some people have searched for happiness through the acquisition of things. Status, success and self worth are measured by how much a person has compared to others in similar positions. Others have tried to find the way out of their lostness through self improvement. Therefore, there is a proliferation of psychological "How to Books," all promising the answer. These have met with mixed success. Still others are in search of happiness, as if happiness is something that one can purchase or find out there somewhere. There are those who are examples of Freud's "Pursuit of Pleasure." However, the lostness and the loneliness remain. During the '70s and the '80s the search went on. Outside there must be some answers. Outside there must be a way. Outside there must be happiness. Yet outside there are no answers, no solutions, no meaning. So for many the search turned inward. There is a searching deep within the spirit, exploring the intangibles, the depths of the spirit, for some answers and a way out, to a more effective life and relationships in the world.

Over the course of the last several years, I have watched and listened to dozens of people in AA as they expressed their lostness and shared their pilgrimage out of the profound lostness. I have felt a kindred spirit with those who have admitted that they alone cannot find the way out. Because of their common disease, they have joined with other people in one of the most profound spiritual journeys of modern time. Together with other searchers they can explore the things that have not worked and maybe, just maybe, they can find some things that do work.

Ten years ago, spirituality, for me personally, seemed to be a good thing for the mystics and pietists; however, spirituality and good Lutheran theology seemed to have little in common. What was important was to know and to understand theological and biblical principles. The more theological people were, obviously the more solidly Christian they would become. The pastor was to impart sage instruction, to teach others what and how to believe, to impart new and wonderful insights on Christian doctrine and teachings.

I began the Doctor of Ministry program because I wanted to be more clinical and psychological. It was in these disciplines that people could find the help they needed. It was here that a solution could be found. The tools of the experts, the psychologists and the psychiatrists, would be of great help. However, the journey has taken me places I never thought possible. Through my association and work with Paul Swanson who has integrated spirituality and theory of personalities; through readings of M. Scott Peck, Merle Jordon, Robert Ackerman, Alice Miller, Jay Haley, and others; through my own counseling experiences, especially through my contact with a number of people in AA, new insights and directions and a new spirituality have begun to evolve. There is a new discovery of a spirituality that is providing a way out of the woods.

M. Scott Peck begins his book, *The Road Less Traveled*, with the simple statement "Life is Difficult."[1] Then he goes on to explain that the happiest and the healthiest are those who have come to an understanding of what that statement means. They know pain and suffering. They do not expect the world to give them a soft way through. Rather they are people who have found a way through the greatest difficulties of life.

9

There is a correlation in the spiritual life as well. Spirituality is difficult. There is no easy way. The growth in spiritual life involves pain and suffering. It is a lifelong process that one enters with great uncertainty and reservations. Because it is difficult there are those who forever stand at the beginning of the journey, but never able to start. There are those who search the spiritual roadmap and try to find another way around. There are those who start the journey and try to turn around, and wait for a later date or better time. The spiritual journey is a road that is also less traveled.

In a speech titled, "Further Along the Road Less Traveled," Scott Peck used the imagery from the garden of Eden to describe the lostness of humankind. He describes the new self awareness Adam and Eve experienced after tasting the fruit of the tree. This becomes a symbol of their consciousness of lostness. Because of their estrangement from God, the unity, wholeness, communion with God, self, and nature were forever to be an elusive pursuit. Then Peck goes on to say that from the garden the people of God were banished to the wilderness. There they were forced to wander for forty years. He says that the desert is a powerful symbol of the existential dilemma that everyone faces. Once in the desert, the Israelites could not return. They had to move forward. But it was through that experience that the Israelites gained a deeper level of consciousness.

Coming to a consciousness of one's desert lostness is the beginning of the spiritual journey. Spirituality is really the search to find a way through the lostness. It is a learning how to deal with the pain of the desert. Contemporary people face their own lostness. They are lost in prejudice, lost in narrow minded cultural customs, lost in self-centered quests, lost in a moral vacuum, lost in decisions in a conflicting value system, and lost in sinful inclination. In a world that is filled with so much lostness, there is a real yearning to find a way out. In a very real way those who use and abuse alcohol or other drugs, are trying to deal with their sense of lostness. If they get the right quantity of alcohol in just the right combination, there is a temporary regained sense of foundness. But it lasts only until the effects of alcohol wear off. As Scott Peck has noted, there is no way of going back; there is only the option of going forward. Those who experience psychological disorders and spiritual disorders, are those who try to return from where they began. The choice of spirituality is the decision to go through the desert and go through the difficulty of lostness. Yes, it is uncomfortable, and even downright painful at times. Yes, there are times that a person would just as soon quit as go on. Yes, there is a temptation to find another answer, an easier answer. Spirituality is the only way to find the way out of the existential lostness.

Those who are in AA have experienced a lostness that few others can come close to. Through the years there were many different theories and solutions given for those who were suffering from alcoholism. Many in the helping professions and even the church saw the alcoholic as a social outcast and a moral reprobate. They offered little hope or promise for those who were chronically dependent on this drug. It wasn't until 1935 that a spiritual approach was offered as a possible solution for this "untreatable disease." And from that point forward Alcoholics Anonymous has been known as a spiritual program. It is the spiritual emphasis of the program that one finds a promise of health and restoration of wholeness.

The founder of AA was significantly affected by Christian doctrines, a specific Christian group, namely, the Oxford Group, and Christian spirituality. Yet at some point in his life he had been turned off by the Christian formal religion and Christian institution called the church. Therefore, he intentionally kept his and the group's distance from anything that closely resembled the church. Yet, he brought so much into AA from the church.

Today there can be a positive result in the reversal of roles. AA has some important things it can teach the church. One of the real attractions of AA, and the reason it continues to be so successful, is that it teaches a wisdom for life that is both good psychology and good spirituality.

That combination could also benefit the church because the church today is in an identity crisis. It is seeking to define itself in new and different ways. In an effort to become relevant and to find its new identity it has adopted and adapted to much of the culture around it. In a pluralistic culture the church is no longer the one voice that everyone turns to for direction. It is one voice among many, and a greatly diminished voice at that. Churches are losing people at an alarming rate. People no longer find meaning and direction from the traditional style and approach of most churches. There is something missing. In an effort to become relevant, the church has given up its traditional religious language. In an effort to regain some of its lost prestige, the church has tried to lead people to a new social consciousness. In an effort not to offend anyone, the church has tried to become all things to all people.

AA has often been called a "religionless spirituality." It is intentionally set up that way. Yet, there is room for spirituality in religion, specifically the Christian religion. For this to happen there has to be some drastic changes in today's Christian Church. It will take changes in attitude, changes in approaches, changes in form, changes in understanding how important spirituality is to the life and growth of the Church.

Deep within the AA tradition are roots which come from the basic core of primitive Christianity. These roots became central as the basic hope for those suffering from the malady of alcoholism.

From early on, those who were drawn together to cope and construct new lives did so by finding an openness to this deeply spiritual approach. It was their last hope. For many of those early alcoholics, they were at the end of their rope. All other alternatives had been tried. This was a last ditch effort to conquer a disease that was all consuming and over which they had no power and were helpless. No, it did not come all at once, as true spirituality never does. Nor did it come without great pain, because saying yes to spirituality means saying no to some other things. Neither did it come as a single clear revelation. Most spiritual journeys are a matter of trial and error with

12

a tremendous amount of blind faith, willingness, and open-mindedness on the part of the searcher. However, it can come and it will work. Now perhaps it is time for the Christian Church to learn from the discipline. We need to learn what it means to be spiritual and to apply a spiritual program to daily living twenty-four hours at a time. I believe the challenge for the '90s for the church is to regain lost spirituality. It is the hope that spirituality is a corrective to religion, a religion that seems to have lost its way, but refuses to ask any of the others that we meet in the forest if they have any way out. Scott Peck says that when people look back at the 20th century one hundred years from now, they will remember that one of the most important events of the twentieth century occurred in 1935 in Akron, Ohio, when Bill W founded the first AA group. If that is true then the influence and contributions of this new tradition will have far reaching effects for more than just those who are affected directly by this disease. It can have a profound effect on the Christian Church as well. AA and the other twelve step programs can teach the church a great deal about how this works and what it can mean.

Chapter 2

The Search Begins

One of the signs of our times and culture is the fact that spirits are so readily available. It gives the impression that here in the bottle or can, are the spirits that people so desperately want and need. In their search to find a way out of the woods hundreds of thousands of people have sought the "Spirit" through the distilled spirits so widely promoted. But their stories tell of lostness, despair, alienation, loneliness, and estrangement.

It is easy to see how alcoholics have lifted bottled spirits to ultimate concern. In fact, it was Dr. William Silkworth in the early '30s, who first described alcoholism as an allergy of the body and a compulsion of the mind. Dr. Silkworth provided Bill Wilson with an understanding of alcohol, "an understanding that offered some choice between founded hope and utter despair, but that left no chance for any vapid middle."[1]

It is that obsession that really sparks the search. It is that obsession that grants god-like power to the object of obsession. This seems to be true whether the obsession is work, or money, or sex or self or whatever else becomes the object of ultimate concern. That obsession grants tremendous power to the obsessed. It is a power that can rule and govern a life in either a positive or negative way. People would like to think that they can control the obsession, that they can keep the obsession bottled, and set it on the shelf and pull it out only when wanted. One of the important lessons learned from AA is that all are on a journey, all are searching for the Holy Grail, all are looking for the Spirit that can touch, move, and guide the inner spirit. The trouble is that people think they can control the Spirit, that the Spirit will respond according to individual will and whims, and that the Spirit is a self serving, self gratifying activity. That's what gets people into trouble psychologically, relationally, and spiritually.

In the Old Testament, the prophets were always fighting false gods. It seemed a part of a primitive culture and society. People assumed they have gotten far beyond worship of golden calves, Baals, and statues created for various gods. In a certain sense the prophets had it easier. People acknowledged their gods, they made objects of the gods they worshiped, and there was a definite sense in which one could tangibly hold and challenge the false gods in their lives. The only way to prove which god had the most power was to put them side by side in an equal match, or wait and see which god spoke the truth by the outcome of events of time and the course of history. Sometimes God answered and acted in ways that brought great fame and recognition both to the Lord and His followers. At other times God remained silent, and in the silence of God, the voices of the other gods crept in. There were times when God would act in ways contrary to what was perceived to be in the best interest of the people. However, the false gods always promised what the hearers wanted.

The gods of this world today are just as powerful and just as prevalent. Today's gods are worshipped with as much fervor and intensity as those of the ancient Canaanites, Egyptians, or Babylonians. Today's gods' claims of success, fame and well-being are equally powerful, if not more so. However, people have tried to deny their existence, and pretend they are not there. Yet these unseen gods have tremendous power to control thinking, behavior, attitudes and relationships. The Old Testament prophets knew their opponent and could point to that opponent and tell people "this is the thing that is destructive to you." Today the gods are unseen, and so they are thought not to have power over people. They are regarded as outdated, and thought to have no relevance for modern man.

16

Everybody has an operational theology. Whether one is Christian, or Buddhist, agnostic, or even atheist, there is a god, a higher power or power greater than oneself, that is the reference point that informs thoughts, decisions, and behaviors. There is a theology. In James Fowler's instrumental work, *Stages of Faith*, he contended that everyone has a faith system.

> *Prior to our being religious or irreligious, before we come to think of ourselves as Catholics, Protestants, Jews, or Muslims, we are already engaged with issues of faith. Whether we become nonbelievers, agnostics or atheists, we are concerned with how to put our lives together and with what will make life worth living. Moreover, we look for something to love that loves us, something to value that gives us value, something to honor and respect that has power to sustain our being.*[2]

Faith is more than believing the Christian doctrine of God revealed in Jesus Christ. Faith is that operational theology that each person bases his or her life upon, and by which one lives and moves and has his or her being. Merle Jordon in his book, *Taking on the Gods*, spoke of the difference between professed theology and operational theology. Professed theology is all those things that people say they believe are true. This is doctrine that is passed down from parents, Sunday School teachers, from any source outside of self, that has told the person, "this is what to believe." The person has said, "yes, it is so" with the lips, but not necessarily in heart and life. A person's operational theology directs not only one's thinking and speaking about God, the world, what is real and what is important and what is not, but more importantly, operational theology directs one's acting and behavior. "Operational theology refers to the implicit religious story by which one is living, including unconscious material."[3]

Some time back a young woman in our congregation called the church office. She began the conversation by describing how things in her life and marriage were all wrong. As she went on to share what was happening, she told me that her husband had just left her again. She believed he was a worthless, lazy, irresponsible person. As she went on I realized what her operational belief system really was. Everything was happening to her. "My husband ran up a lot of bills because he knew what it would do to me." "My parents have taken his side," she said. "Do you know what that has done to me? My children are constantly misbehaving because they are trying to get to me." Then she lashed out at God. "Yeah, God, Ha! What has God ever done for me? You preachers tell us to believe that God is a loving God — some loving God He is that would make this stuff happen to me. All my life I was taught the 10 commandments and love your neighbor crap. Look what that stuff has done for me." This woman had been drinking most of the afternoon when she made the call. Her family had planned, but failed, at an intervention in order to try to get her into treatment. She was near the bottom but not quite there yet. She had a professed belief system that was in direct conflict with her operational belief system.

We are learning to understand that for the alcoholic, the bottle has become the godlike power in that person's life. For the alcoholic there is a real struggle to take hold of and control the spirit they are so desperately seeking. As one carefully listens to an alcoholic person, they will provide all kinds of clues to what is really the ultimate controlling spirit in their life.

The "U" Chart first developed by Dr. Jellinek in 1952 is foundational for this paper. It was a part of his study of more than two thousand chronic alcoholics that revealed the distinct stages in the progression and the recovery of the disease of alcoholism. The chart is included at the end of this book. No one becomes an alcoholic overnight. It is a progressive disease that gradually takes control over a long period of time. It first starts with the occasional relief drinking. From that point, there is an increasing use and focus on the bottled spirits. Coupled with the increase in drinking is a change in behavior and one's inner emotional thinking and feeling. As one moves to the chronic phase of drinking, there is less and less control over one's life and a continual withdrawal from others. Behavior, emotions, and feelings, in turn, suffer. Without help, life for the alcoholic continues to deteriorate. At some point there is a bottoming out. It is out of this bottoming out experience, out of the total defeat that a new beginning can take place. A new life and dramatic change toward health comes when the alcoholic comes to that awareness that Scott Peck talks about in the lostness. At that point there is a sincere desire for help. One of the earliest signs of recovery is that a person's spiritual needs are examined. As one recovers from the disease, there is a reconnection with family and friends, there is a reorganization of thinking and feeling, and there is an honest examination and appraisal of who one is and where they are going. The higher one heads up the road of recovery, the higher one travels toward attaining love, happiness and joy.

Tim Fellers, who is the Chemical Dependency Program Coordinator at Partners in Psychiatry, developed the same chart that also tracks alcoholism as a spiritual disease, both in its progression and recovery. It, too, is included at the end of this book. That format is the inspiration and the guideline in this paper to pull together twelve steps that are essential in spiritual recovery and growth and consistent and central to the Christian faith and life. Because alcoholism is a spiritual disease it would seem natural that there are some spiritual signs and symptoms as one comes to an awareness of the power of this disease and its effects. As one looks at the deterioration that comes in one's spirituality one can see that there is a distancing from God and there is an estrangement from self and others that could be described as the lostness suggested in the first chapter. The sicker one gets physically, the sicker one becomes spiritually. Out of the mist of the lostness, comes this vague notion, that life can be different and it can be better. As the reader can see, I have picked out and picked up on many of the stages of the spiritual recovery process and used them as steps to spirituality in this book.

What is true in the alcoholic is true in all of us to greater or lesser degree. We are all defined by what we perceive to be the ultimate authority in our lives. We live out our experiences being defined by that ultimate authority. Merle Jordon has put it this way:

Self concept always goes hand-in-hand with one's concept of ultimate authority; the doctrine of personhood is always related to the doctrine of God, whether one is avowedly religious or not. Thus the question of identity that is usually asked in our time — Who am I? — is not helpful outside of the relational question, Whose am I? Self is always defined in terms of Other or of a false 'Other.'[4]

The beginning of spiritual awareness and growth comes from an honest examination and evaluation of what is the god or gods that really govern one's operational theology. Are they the same or different from people that profess to believe? As people peel each layer back, they get closer and closer to the center of their belief system, which so pervasively and persuasively defines them and their actions. Deep down within each person is a god. That god is the one that will define, move, direct, shape and control personality, relationships and world view.

Throughout the Old Testament, the Israelites spoke of the God of Abraham, Isaac, and Jacob. Part of that was cultural honor given to ancient ancestors. But more than that it was a spiritual reference point to see if the same god the Israelites were following today was the god of Abraham, Isaac, and Jacob. If not, there was a problem. The problem was not with God, but with how they were relating or not relating to the one true God. What was true then, is equally true now. There are many gods competing for allegiance, devotion and worship. These gods offer many promises. They promise power, success, wealth, happiness, and a whole host of things that people desire. More often than not, these gods are of our own making. They are reflections of human characteristics and values. As people live in relation to these gods, meaning and purpose, value and understanding are given. As a person's god is, so they will be. Those who follow the God of Abraham, Isaac, and Jacob will be far different in their relationships and values than those who follow other gods.

People's spiritual journeys are always an inward journey, and then there is an outward expression of what has taken place inside. People who are truly spiritual are focused, centered and grounded. They are also empathetic, compassionate, self-giving and forgiving of others. Jesus spoke of building one's house upon the rock and Paul spoke of establishing a solid foundation. They knew that it would be so easy to focus and ground one's life on the wrong things. At the same time Jesus spoke of serving and reaching the least and the lost and Paul spoke of embodying love and sharing each others' joys and burdens. They knew that the value of spirituality had outward direction as well.

Self esteem and self identity are always related to what is at the deepest level of a person's life. Self esteem has to do with one's own personal self-image. The Bible says that humans are created in the image of God. That is true. It is true on two levels. On an absolute level each person is created in the image of the God who created the heavens and the earth. But on another level persons are created in the image of the god whom they relate to and give allegiance to. For some it is money, others a bottle, others a parental authority figure, for others it is control and power. Even though these are false gods they still have incredible power to shape and define people. There can be no changes in self-image until there is a foundational and fundamental change in the god a person relates to. No one can change a single thing about what they believe about self, their self-image, or even self-esteem, until they first honestly deal (because delusion is so easy here) with the ultimate authority who is guiding their life. As Merle Jordon puts it: "I believe that it is imperative for pastoral counselors to understand the idolatry that lies at the heart of most pathology. A person's erroneous view of self is interwoven with that person's erroneous view of God."[5]

The thing that makes the AA story so powerful is that the movement to wholeness and healing came directly out of such a struggle and experience. The alcoholic's battle is a fight over who will be the god of his life. Will it be the Higher power-God or the higher power-Self? Both make competing claims of being the individual's higher power. It has been through the work of AA that people have become aware of the undeniable power and claim that the self has on a situation or person. In the history of the story of the founder of AA, Bill W's profound revelation came when he found that he was not God. It was only when he came to that realization that he could take the first step toward health. When he discovered that he was not God he begin to rid himself from the bottled spirits that kept him out of touch with the true Spirit that he was so desperately searching for. "Two intermingled themes brought Bill Wilson to the verge of the ultimate, recognized founding moment: the hopelessness of the condition of the alcoholic, and the necessity of an experience of conversion."[6]

Sydney J. Harris, the insightful columnist for the Chicago Daily News, once wrote a column "Spurring our Better Selves." In it he made the observation that self improvement and self control do not come as a result of having the right philosophy or believing the right doctrine. He said, "Millions of people call themselves Christians and believe every item of the Apostle's Creed, but in their daily lives they are as far removed from the gospel of Jesus as if they had never heard of Him." Real direction and control of life come from following the example of one who has walked before a person whom that person respects and seeks to emulate. Jesus taught many things, but His greatest teaching was by the example that He provided for all of His followers, both past and present. The real power of Jesus came through His actions, and His actions have affected and changed the direction and the actions of countless millions of people throughout history. As Harris states,

> *We can draw strength and righteousness only from another person, from someone we perceive to be better than we are, to be more of what a person was meant to be. When we find such a person — and he or she can always be found if we look hard enough — we must use that person as a touch stone for testing the truth of our own behavior.*

In AA that being can be the AA group as a whole, a higher power, or another respected person such as a sponsor. Bill W found what ancient Christians found before him and what the Israelites found before that, that one's spiritual journey is best expressed not in theological categories, or profound religious doctrines, or even in professed belief systems. It is best found in story. For it is in the story of one's life that one can begin to see not only "Who a person is" but more importantly "Whose he is." That story, like a fingerprint, is unique to that person. There is no one else with exactly the same experiences, the same personality, the same position in the family, the same anything. That's why testimonies have been so important in the growth and life of AA and also the Church. That is why, when asked to explain how AA works, Bill W told his story. Perhaps that is why, when Jesus was asked about the Kingdom of God, and what it meant to be a follower, He told a story. And that is why, when trying to describe one's own spiritual journey, it is best when it is done as a story.

One of the earliest tenets of AA is "it works." But one had to make it work. Like anything else there was no magic. It takes practice and participation. There is no explanation, except the invitation to keep coming back. What counted was the results seen in the lives of people who were changed. True spirituality is like that — it works. How or why it works will probably never be perfectly clear. But it does work if consistently applied to life and daily living. It takes willingness and commitment to the practice. Far too often people are looking for a magical spirituality. That will never happen. Spiritual growth takes time, effort, discipline and commitment.

There are practices to be exercised if solid spirituality is to become a reality. I am not sure if there can ever be written down a single set of "how to's" that will fit every person. Spirituality doesn't come in a canned program that one can follow like an instruction booklet. Spirituality is too big and too vague until it can be broken down into smaller parts. What follows are twelve parts or steps, similar to the steps of AA. If these twelve steps are applied in a consistent and conscientious way they can lead to greater spiritual growth for those who apply them.

Chapter 3

Step One:
Crisis

Before one takes the first step in spirituality, there has to be a reason to get involved. In some way or another the person who is going to be moving toward spirituality has to be in a crisis or conflict. Where and how the crisis comes about seems to matter little, only that the person can no longer get along with former coping mechanisms. When there is no crisis or conflict, any attitude or belief system will work. However, when a person is put in a crisis, all resources are called up and the defenses are readied. The internal coping mechanisms are put in gear. As long as the crisis is not too great, as long as the conflict is solvable with the thinking and feelings that are already in place, there is no reason to change. However, if the crisis is long enough, if it is severe enough, if it is uncomfortable enough, then something must change.

Perhaps pastors have regarded these crises and conflicts as bad and as a threat to spirituality and spiritual growth. They have given lip service to the value of a strong faith to enable one to get through the messes of life. But there is a real fear that when crises come along they might just blow the person right out of the spiritual waters. That might be so, since there are no guarantees in this spiritual pilgrimage. However, great Christians have been shaped by their crisis which in the long run provided a strong spiritual center that guided their thinking, formed their values and motivated their living.

Rabbi Harold Kushner has written, *When Bad Things Happen To Good People*,[1] which is a remarkably perceptive work on his own personal struggle to give meaning to undeserved suffering. When Kushner's son was diagnosed with a rare childhood disease, it threw the Kushners into a real spiritual quandary. Pat answers no longer had any meaning, worn out cliches were severely disturbing, pious platitudes were not comforting and were perceived as offensive. The crisis of his son's illness and death sent the Kushners back into the Scriptures searching for answers and for a way to make sense out of what had happened. Kushner said that he reread the Book of Job which is God's special gift for those in crisis and suffering. Even though he had read that book for classes at the seminary, and had even written several papers on it, it never spoke to him like it did when he was in his own crisis. No, he would have never chosen this to happen to his son or any other family. That crisis put his family through tremendous pain and hell. One can see today only the results of what the Kushners have experienced and worked through. However, without a doubt, it was that event in their lives that deepened and strengthened their spirit beyond measure.

Without conflict or crisis in life there is no change. AA provides one of the richest paradigms of crisis-motivated spirituality. A friend of mine told me the other day that there has never yet been an alcoholic who has said, "You know, today is a warm and lovely day, everything is bright and beautiful, all is right with me and my God. I think I'll get sober." That's just not the way it happens.

For the alcoholic the bottoming out experience is the crisis that moves him or her toward treatment and wholeness. I talked to a young man who had been in treatment for the third time. He said that he was sick and tired of being sick and tired. Yet after each time in the treatment center he would come out, be better for a while, then return to his old way and patterns of thinking and acting. Even though he said he wanted to change, the old self-survival techniques he had learned so well just took over any of the new stuff he had learned. He would talk of his Higher Power and living for to-day, of taking care of himself. Yet there was such a difference between his attitudes, actions and words. Finally, he relapsed. It was worse than before. The test results came back on the liver and the doctor told him that if he drank again he would be dead. What he said was profound, "I have at least one more drunk in me; however, I'm not sure I have one more recovery in me."

Jesus was not afraid of conflict, either at a personal level or an interpersonal level. In a very real way, it was the conflicts with the scribes and Pharisees that really allowed Him to define Himself and His mission. The temptations in the wilderness were a crisis of where He should place His allegiance and in whom. The question of, "Who do you say I am?" was a crisis of identity, if not for Jesus, then for the disciples. The Garden of Gethsemane experience also was a crisis of follow through. After praying that the cup might pass from him, Jesus returned to where the disciples were sleeping, and asked, "Could you not watch me one hour?" When Jesus was questioned by the Pharisees re: "Who does your allegiance go to? Which is the greatest law? Who will be married in heaven?" He was put in crisis. Each and every crisis, large or small, helped Jesus redefine Himself, His mission and His relation to the Father. Not only that, Jesus created His own conflicts in the lives of people. Perhaps it would be interesting to read the Gospels from the point of crisis creation and resolution. Jesus' healing on the Sabbath created conflict. His rhetorical questions upset the status quo. His directives — "go, sin no more, forgive seven times seventy, sell all that you have, go and do likewise," put people in a crisis that they had to respond to either positively or negatively. His association and identification with the sick, poor, and outcast created conflict internally and interpersonally. His statements about not bringing peace but a sword and family members being against each other were very upsetting.

Jesus brought conflict. His presence often created a crisis which ultimately lead to the cross. There were those who battled

Him and refused to leave their set courses and comfort zones. There were those who ran from the challenge. There were those who were changed, often dramatically and significantly, by the crisis Jesus brought. No longer could they think the same way, or act or feel the same as before. Their attitude and outlook dramatically changed.

The Alban Institute sponsors seminars on Conflict and Conflict Management. They believe that every organization needs some conflict to keep it going and to move it toward the growing edge. Too much conflict obviously can be destructive but, by the same token, too little conflict can be equally harmful. Where there is conflict there also is a growing edge. Conflict brings pain with it and there is no growth without pain.

The same is true in family therapy. The job of the family therapist is to infuse just enough conflict in the family system to keep it off balance. As the conflict increases and intensifies so does the anxiety level. When the anxiety level gets high enough then there is possibility of change.

In co-dependent relationships there is an investment in keeping the alcoholic out of crisis. The family goes to any and all ends not to allow the alcoholic to take responsibility. They work hard at being over adequate. They try to maintain normalcy — whatever that might be. They pay a big price for taking care of the family in the roles they play and in the energy they expend.

What keeps people out of crisis? Denial keeps people out of crisis. What a powerful emotion that is. Denial says the person has no problem. The person says, "I'm ok. It must be you. It must be them. It certainly isn't my fault." Denial does two contradictory things; one outside the person and the other inside the person. The founders of AA found denial to be one of the most powerful of human emotions. Denial, as Ernest Kurtz noted,

> tended to be expressed in especially two contrary insistences: the 'claim to be able to drink like other people'; and the 'exceptional thinking' that insisted that even though the problem-drinker's outward experience seemed

*to place him in the alcoholic camp, he was somehow
'different.'*[2]

People can live in denial for years. The world can be crumbling around them, and yet they maintain the denial system.

Grandiosity certainly keeps people out of crisis. "I am more than I really am. I am better than I really am." It is the inflated ego of the macho rugged individualist who creates this false image that he is totally self-sufficient. Delusional thinking makes the self God and prevents any kind of profound honesty about personal weakness. If the person cannot come to terms with the fact that they are not God, there is little hope of emotional, or spiritual growth.

Decadence, too, keeps people out of crisis. This does not necessarily mean one is morally corrupt or a terrible person. The dictionary defines decadence as "an eroding, growing worse, decline." In an alcoholic family the old adage is, "it will probably get worse before it gets better." In an alcoholic family much of what happens in other families is only amplified and intensified. Because alcoholism is a degenerative and progressive disease, the decline and degeneration of every part of the family is evident. Yet those involved may choose to ignore it.

Deceit is another thing that keeps people out of crisis. They live in a deceptive world. There are deceptive rationalizations that all is OK. Alcoholics are masters of deception. If the great work of satan is deception, then alcoholic families live in a fantasy world until reality can no longer be put off. M. Scott Peck speaks quite extensively of the power of deception in the book, *People of the Lie.*[3] According to him, what separates evil from normal sins is that those who are trapped by evil refuse to allow the truth to speak to them. A speaker at an AA meeting once said, "The truth will set you free. But before it does it will probably piss you off."

Defensiveness is another emotional reaction that keeps people out of crisis. Whatever is said can be warded off by a defensive person. Whatever is directed toward the person can be deflected away. Whatever challenges are made can quickly be turned around. Defensive people are often in conflict but never in crisis. They never allow themselves to be open long enough to entertain or experience change. It is usually the case that the more defensive a person is the greater the likelihood they were hurt. That which they are most defensive about is what will arouse the most resistance.

There are other things that can keep people out of crisis or conflict. But there is always a price to pay. Sometimes people can delay and deny what is at issue for months and even years, however at some point in time the crisis will resurface in a way that will have to be dealt with.

One tends to be very skeptical about people who say that they have never had a doubt. Faith and spirituality are far more difficult than that. People who never have a doubt probably are still functioning with the faith of their parents or some other authority figure. They never have been challenged enough, or have never had to dig into their own resources to find out what they really believe. In other words, nothing has come along to help them become separated and individualized from what father, mother or some other authority in life has to say.

Some people are able to recite wonderful Bible passages. They can tell you precise, accurate, ecclesiastical doctrine. They can stand up and speak eloquently about God. However, it is difficult to try to pin them down to what they personally believe. They need to get out from behind the spiritual systems of others. This is not to say that people cannot learn a lot from others. It is only to say that people cannot live out, and believe another person's system. Dr. William James wrote his monumental classic, *Varieties of Religious Experience*,[4] some 80 years ago. Bill W received this book as a gift from his friend, Ebby. This book had such a profound effect on Bill W that it became a life changing force for him and also one of the influential points of the new movement. In fact, it was called the third of the four founding moments of AA.[5] William James spoke of religious experience from a psychological standpoint and not just a religious perspective, which is what made it so appealing to Bill W. There, he talked of basically two types of religious experience. One was healthy and the other was sick. It was almost ironic how his description of great religious experience involved those people who suffered with torn consciences, and who struggled daily with the presence and absence of God in their lives. Spiritual experiences, according to James, had the common denominator of pain, suffering, calamity, complete hopelessness, and deflation of the self. Those in-depth experiences were required to make one receptive and ready for a new and powerful spiritual experience.

Anton Boisen's classic work, *The Exploration Of The Inner World*,[6] is his autobiographical account of his personal struggle with spirituality that came out of his own depression. Each depression episode was followed by a growth in spirituality.

Martin Luther was driven into the priesthood by his own angst — a fear of his father that he transferred to his fear of God. Most of Luther's life could be written from the perspective of conflict with others in authority and crisis in his own internal faith life. It was only as he experienced and embraced God's grace and unconditional love that he could find release from his torment. Without conflict and crisis Luther would have remained in obscurity and the Reformation probably would never have happened.

Biblically, Job is the classic example of a man facing crisis. He is a man of faith, with no problems and everything going his way. Then, one day he loses it all. It takes only two chapters for the stage to be set and the tragedy to beset Job. Thirty-nine chapters are spent describing the conflict and crisis. Scripture describes the very personal and dramatic struggle of what this means. When he finally comes to the resolution, he can say, "I know, Lord, that you are all-powerful; that you can do everything you want. You told me to listen while you spoke . . . I knew only what others had told me, but now I have seen you with my own eyes. So I am ashamed of all I have said and repent in dust and ashes." The emphasis is on "My." Faith is not secondhand or something that can be imparted by even his best friends. His crisis had allowed him to see God with his own eyes. Out of this experience, out of the depth of his soul Job has found the saving grace of God's presence.

Conflicts and crisis will come. They can be evaded and avoided but they can be faced and welcomed as opportunities to enter into the spiritual journey that will ultimately lead in our spiritual life to new strength and balance and integrity, all of which are essentials of a healthy spirituality.

Chapter 4

Step Two: Surrender

As a youth I was both on the giving end and the receiving end of some fights with my brother and classmates. Those were the days in which the fights never ended in more than a bloody nose, but they were fights to establish dominance and a pecking order. Most often the fight would end up in a wrestling match, with the winner being on top of the loser. The guy on top would yell, "Say uncle." "Never," was the reply. Then a little more pressure: "Say uncle." "Never!" Finally more pressure yet, so that the bottom guy was in an absolutely hopeless, helpless state. Pain was always an effective means of effecting the response of, "Uncle, uncle. I give up, I give up."

Probably the most important step in spiritual growth in life is this step called surrender. People hate it because it reminds them too often of all those humiliating experiences that they had as children, when they were down on the ground with someone sitting on their chest, pinning them to the ground with their knees which left hands free to slap or hit at will.

At the Appomattox Court House, on April 9, 1865, General Robert E. Lee surrendered to General Grant to end the Civil War. It is a peaceful place. It has become a symbol of peace, and reunification of the union, and the opportunity for a new start. But it took five years of bloody war to get to Appomattox. Hundreds of thousands on both sides were killed. The land was scarred for generations by the battles that were fought on both sides of the Mason-Dixon Line, and vast amounts of resources were poured into the conflict on both sides before an armistice could take place. So much happened before the surrender on that April day of 1865. A victory here or there did not bring about the surrender. Only when the Union Army marched south, destroying the heart of Dixie; only after southern supplies of food and ammunition were exhausted; only when there was total domination of every sector and the overwhelming superiority of Northern troops firmly established in every area of the South; did Lee sit down and sign the papers of surrender.

In the stories people tell in AA, each and every one is about the war they were in with alcohol. It is what one book has so aptly named, *The Booze Battle*. From the first drink on, the war was on. For most, they held the upper hand for years. But slowly, ever so slowly, the tide of the Battle began to tip against them. As the war continued, more drinking erupted. At first, the drinker was satisfied that he could handle whatever number of drinks were fired at him. In the beginning the worst losses were the embarrassments of what was done while drunk and the persistent hangovers. Before fully getting over them, they were called into battle again. As the tide of the war began to switch in the alcohol's favor, the drinker called in new re-inforcements. These were allies, new recruits — denial, dishonesty, deceptive hiding, resentment. But alcohol brought in its reserves as well. Powerful forces, these regiments of alcohol, including shame, guilt, depression, anger. Denial, deception, and dishonesty are tremendous allies in the war effort. They can aid in the illusionary victories of many battles against alcohol and its gang of forces. Ultimately, as powerful as they are, they are no match for the forces of alcohol. The battles are waged in the body. The physical effects and the scars left both inside and outside of a person are many. Some of these wounds will never heal. There is considerable damage to the mind. Because alcoholism was and is a compulsion of the mind as well an allergy of the body, it affects much of the thinking which disrupts the communication lines of thinking and feeling. During the time the person was drinking, alcohol was sending raiding parties to the thinking and feeling communication lines to disrupts, distort and interrupt the normal processing of information.

But the greatest damage is done to the spirit. In looking for someone to put in charge of this new confederacy, no better candidate could be found than the self. Even though the self lacked a lot of the qualifications to run something as important as the life of a person, the self became enamored with the power and the prestige that being president conferred. The self became controlling, authoritarian, and powerful. As the battle waged on, the self would not relinquish an ounce of control, or one bit of the grandeur, that came from being in command. Even at the bitter end, when the world around was crumbling and falling apart, self would not let go. "I would rather die than surrender." Some do it that way.

But the war is not easily ended. There are those who say they need to surrender, but have not made the decision to do so. Sometimes they pretend to surrender only to get up and fight again. There are those who surrender for others in order to buy time so they can figure out a new way to carry on the war. There are those who want a cease fire. They even stop the battling. They want to dictate the terms of surrender, in which keeping self in control and authority is a top concern.

The effects of the battles of the war can be seen in the alcoholic, his family, and other areas of his life. It is easy to stand on the outside in judgement without ever entering into an empathetic understanding of the person who is waging a war for the control of his life. Suggestions from outsiders are usually met with resistance and defiance until the person himself is ready to surrender. Tiebout gives an understanding of why this carries on:

> Defiance my be defined as that quality which permits the individual who has it to snap his fingers in the face of reality and live on 'unperturbed.' It has two special values for handling life situations whether inner or outer. In the first place, defiance, certainly with alcoholics, is a surprisingly effective tool for managing anxiety or reality which is so often a source of anxiety. If you defy a fact

and say it it not so and can succeed in doing so unconsciously, you can drink to the day of your death, forever denying the imminence of that fate.[1]

Bo tells about the day when his family met in a doctor's office. There in the room, when he walked in, was his wife and four kids. Even though he was high at the time, it never crossed his mind that they might be there for him and his problem because he didn't think he had a problem. His first thought was that there must be something wrong with one of the kids. When they each in turn told him of their love for him and their pain because of his drinking, he said he melted and that was it. That was his Appomattox, his "crying uncle," his surrender.

Oh, if surrendering were that easy. Certainly people need to be aware of the battles, wounds and scars prior to, but also after the surrender. Surrendering is an event. There is a point in time and place, when a person says, "this is it, I can't go on like this anymore. I can't live like this. My world is destroyed and devastated. Now is the time to surrender."

Yet there are always two very powerful forces vying for control up to the bitter end. On one side, the defiant part believes it can manage the drinking. On the other side, the facts speak loudly and with increasing insistence to the contrary. On one side, grandiosity claims there is nothing it cannot master and control and, on the other side, the facts demonstrate unmistakably the opposite. The dilemma of the alcoholic is now obvious. His unconscious mind rejects through its capacity for defiance and grandiosity what his conscious mind perceives. "Hence, realistically, the individual is frightened by his drinking and at the same time is prevented from doing anything about it by the unconscious activity which can and does ignore or override the conscious mind."[2] When the alcoholic surrenders in the face of alcohol he loses the battle over alcohol in order to win the war over alcoholism.

Yet, denial and defiance are powerful forces preventing surrender. This is not just an individual phenomenon, but a family phenomenon as well. Both will try to adapt and cope and limp along rather than surrender.[3] "I don't need help, I'm in control. I can take it. As bad as it is, I really don't want to change. Isn't there some magic wand that can be waved in order to fix him/her? I resent having to do anything. He/she is the one with the problem." People hold on to denial and defiance tenaciously until the end in hopes of being spared the pain of surrender. For a lot of people this is a reliving of childhood pain.

We always have to keep our guard up in the hopes that no one will find out what's really inside, which means that our symptoms are also about shame. They are about the shame of 'being found out,' of being 'discovered,' of being emotionally naked in front of others and being laughed at, criticized or rejected.[4]

It is a way to protect people from reality that is too painful to let into their conscious minds. When denial becomes a way of life, it is disastrous. It blocks people's thinking by the process of rationalization, blaming, excusing and putting off action. It blocks feelings so that people learn to deny, ignore, or try to escape their feelings. Yet the pain is always acted out in one way or another by personal physical problems, by one of the family members getting in trouble, or even by an "unrelated" mental or emotional problem. It affects the spiritual life by looking for God to come in and magically fix everything up so that the person can live happily ever after. It is the delusional thinking that everything will get better in time. John and Linda Friel call this insanity. In fact, they have a great saying for this: "Insanity is doing the same thing and expecting different results."[5]

Not only is surrender an event in space and time, but more importantly it is a process. There is a continual need to surrender if this spiritual program is going to work. Surrender of control is the primary step. In fact, the first three steps of the 12 Step Program of AA deals with the "process" of surrender.

1. We admitted we were powerless over alcohol (event) — that our lives had become unmanageable.

2. We came to realize that a Power Greater than Ourselves could restore us to sanity.

3. We made a decision to turn our will and our lives over to the care of God as we understand Him. (process)

In a 12 Step Program, these steps sometimes take months and years to complete. This is not a one time thing that a person never has to return to once they are completed. People need to retrace these steps and to remember to work through these steps continually, as they move toward greater sobriety. Bill W had a solid understanding of this. He observed: "Such is the nature of the human being that I doubt any 100 percent conformity or surrender is possible — the only perfection is in God Himself. All the rest is relative."[6]

It is like taking the steps from the basement to the upstairs of the house. A person has to work through this step every time.

It is so easy to forget these initial steps and feel that one does not have to go back to them. But that denies the power of the self and the ego's desire for regaining self control. A young man in the program said, "I am so happy. Now my self esteem is high, I really feel good about me, but I've always got to keep my ego in check." One of the first things they share in AA is that EGO is the acronym for Easing God Out. The people who cannot keep their ego in check have what Tiebout calls an "enlarged ego." As he explains it, the ego is made up of three persisting elements in the adult psyche of the original nature of the child. In citing Freud, Tiebout explains:

> ... the infant is born ruler of all he surveys. He comes from the Nirvana of the womb, where he is usually the sole occupant, and he clings to that omnipotence with an innocence, yet, determination, which baffles parent after parent. The second, stemming directly from the monarch within, is that the infant tolerates frustration poorly and lets the world know it readily. The third significant aspect of the child's original psyche is its tendency to do everything in a hurry.[7]

It is these surviving qualities of the infantile psyche that lead to feelings of omnipotence, which raises the ego to divinity status, which is accompanied by the inability to accept frustration which threatens the regal status of the ego.

No one wants to "let go and let God." That is completely out of the normative experience of most people. Even now, this idea of surrender is met with a great deal of suspicion and skepticism. People who are looking for sobriety without surrender are just not going to find it. What those in AA have done is reopened an ancient step in the spiritual journey of everyone.

Christians have spoken of surrender for years. But that is such a loaded term. Freud's word association game is kicked into play every time the word surrender is spoken. Say the word surrender to yourself, and what comes to mind immediately? "No way!" "What, are you stupid?" "Weakness?" "Defeat? ..." Every person can probably fill in the blanks with their own responses. There is something within each person that naturally resists the process of surrendering just as stubbornly as an alcoholic resists it.

There is a lot at stake here because, as in war, there are no conditional surrenders, only unconditional ones. There is so much that has to be given up when people surrender, yet there is so much to be gained. Lewis Smedes says that there are three things that people have to give up when they surrender. "We surrender our freedom. We surrender our individuality. We surrender our control."[8] Ironically, surrender brings together a paradoxical combination of love, commitment, and strength. "Committed love is a paradoxical power. Paradoxical? Yes, paradoxical, because it is a power to surrender. A power to surrender? Yes power, because sometimes it takes a lot of strength to surrender."[9] It always takes a lot to surrender.

There is no reason to surrender unless there is some hope that things will be better. That's the difference between helplessness and hopelessness. The reason surrender takes so long and is fought so hard is that people do not see anything better on the other side. In fact, there is a very real fear that there might just not be another side. For the alcoholic the admission of surrender grasps hold of another kind of life and living.

*When that happens, the individual is wide open to reality;
he can listen and learn without conflict and fighting back.
He is receptive to life, not antagonistic. He senses a feeling of relatedness and at-oneness which becomes the
source of an inner peace and serenity, the possession of
which frees the individual from the compulsion to drink.
In other words, an act of surrender is an occasion wherein
the individual no longer fights life, but accepts it."*[10]

There is an important truth about surrender that the
modern mind needs to grasp. M. Scott Peck, in talking about
the paradox of free will says, "There are only two states of
being: submission to God and goodness or the refusal to sub-
mit to anything beyond one's own will — which refusal automatically enslaves one to the forces of evil. We must ultimately
belong either to God or the devil."[11] For those on their spiritual
journey surrendering becomes the most important vital step
of the spiritual life. It is a choosing of God and goodness. It
is the first step toward humility in relation to God and self.

*... this human activity, freely engaged in, which leads
to the salvation of sobriety, consists essentially in a continuing elaboration and amplification of the initial act
of surrender. Thus Alcoholics Anonymous remains true
to its core Evangelical Pietist insights. According to this
insight, which can be expressed in either religious or secu-
lar form, the human activity most fundamentally essential to the attainment of 'salvation' is accepting reality.*[12]

It is the example and the model that Jesus set for the world.
It is in surrendering that God, self and life are brought together
in a new and exciting way. M. Scott Peck has an insightful
way of describing what we have been speaking of here: "I realized that one way or another, no matter what my topic, I am
always trying in whatever way I can to help people take God,
Christ, and themselves far more seriously than they generally
do."[13]

*From the very beginning we are told that God created
us in His own image. Are we going to take that seriously?*

40

Accept the responsibility that we are godly beings? And
that human life is of sacred importance? Speaking of his
relationship to us human beings, Jesus said, 'I have come
that they might have life, and that they might have it more
abundantly.' Abundantly. What a wonderful word![14]

The need to surrender is analogous to the first of the ten commandments. "I am the Lord your God, you shall have no other gods before me." When Martin Luther was asked which was the most important of the ten commandments, he said it was the first, because all the commandments follow this one. If this first commandment is kept, one does not have to worry about keeping the rest. They just naturally take care of themselves. The same is true of surrender for the spiritual life and journey. Psychologically stated:

> *Mental health requires that the human will submit itself*
> *to something higher than itself. To function decently in*
> *this world we must submit ourselves to some principle*
> *that takes precedence over what we might want at any*
> *given moment. For the religious this principle is God, and*
> *so they will say, 'Thy will, not mine, be done.' But if they*
> *are sane, even the nonreligious submit themselves,*
> *whether they know it or not, to some 'higher power' —*
> *be it truth, or love, the needs of others, or the demands*
> *of reality.*[15]

Once one surrenders — truly surrenders — the other stuff seems far easier to do and makes better sense.

Surrendering means giving up power and control no matter how limited or extended that is. Surrendering directly confronts the omnipotence and self grandiosity that is openly characteristic in the alcoholic, but is covertly prevalent in us all. It is what changes one's perception, attitude and stance toward life, both on a conscious and unconscious level. The second question raised here is, How does the surrender reaction change the inner psychic picture?

> *This question is based on a presupposition, namely, that*
> *surrender is an emotional step in which the Ego, at least*

for the time being, acknowledges that it is no longer supreme. This acknowledgment is valueless if limited to consciousness; it must be accompanied by similar feelings in the unconscious. For the alcoholic, surrender is marked by the admission of being powerless over alcohol. His sobriety has that quality of peace and tranquility which makes for a lasting quiet within only if the surrender is effective in the unconscious and permanent as well. [16]

Once the ego is disposed of, the quieted self is made receptive and able to observe what is going on inside the self. It is the beginning of a real inventory. Somehow, some way, the person has to come to terms with the idea that they are NOT GOD. Yet it is so scary to confront the fallacy that people can control their lives. In truth,

We can influence our lives; we cannot control them. Thinking that is based on control leads straight to the addictive process and the disease of co-dependence. When we put ourselves in the driver's seat or play God, we become enmeshed in the addictive system. [17]

When I was in college, I used to have a reoccurring dream. In it I was on a ladder. I was grasping tightly to each and every rung. I never got anywhere because it seemed that I slipped off any rung either higher or lower than where I was standing. The same was true of my hands. I never was able to grab any other rung of the ladder other than the one I now had. It was dark, pitch black. I could not see above nor could I see below. I was scared, for I felt alone. My greatest fear was falling. But at some point in the dream process I finally let go, sure that I was going to fall into nothingness forever. But I didn't. Something held me when I let go. It was amazing. It was a grace experience. It was an unconscious way of showing me what had to be done. What made the dream more powerful is the fact that it persisted at a time when my life was completely out of control. I was failing in college, failing in friendships, and failing in my self identity and self worth.

42

Since that time I have been reminded of that dream often. It was probably the first step in my spiritual searching process thus far.

In a ruggedly, individualistic, narcissistic, power-oriented culture, it is not surprising that surrender of control would be such a difficult step. This is especially true for people who are part of the white dominated cultural milieu. People working in the field of alcohol dependency have been finding that the process of surrender is different for those from a black or a native American cultural setting. There the strength and the power of the family, the culture, and the values of the people are all important in bringing about the surrender and thus the changes. Since their powerlessness is already felt and exhibited in their inferiority and lack of self respect, the disease only amplifies their helplessness. For them surrender is empowerment.[18]

Surrender is basically coming to that new awareness that there is a God. God is not in the bottle, God is not in my controlling, and God is not me. In both a conscious and unconscious way it is admitting we are powerless over people, places and things. It is coming to the humbling knowledge that God has not died and left any individual in charge.

Surrender is that letting go that I felt in the dream. It's the letting go that is spoken about in every AA meeting. It is letting go of the delusional belief system that sets a person up to be the "divine." "As one sees this struggle in process, the need for the helping hand of a Deity becomes clearer. Mere man alone all too often seems powerless to stay the force of his Ego. He needs outside assistance and needs it urgently."[19] AA picked up on the substantial religious truth that salvation is obtained through conversion and by surrender.

> *The admission of the First Step marked acceptance that*
> *'bottom' had been hit. It also echoed a deeper admission*
> *— the irony of 'original sin' as described by the Book*
> *of Genesis. In the Garden of Eden, Adam and Eve had*
> *sinned by reaching for more than had been given. They*
> *ate of the forbidden fruit because the serpent promised*
> *that eating it would make them 'as Gods.'*[20]

Both Adam and Eve and the alcoholic have tried to control reality and have come up hard against human finitude. It is like one alcoholic said, "Everyone used to tell me that I was the kind of guy that lived on the edge. But I didn't know where the edge was." Religiously speaking, freedom of the will was an important part of creation. It is what separates us from other animals. It was a risk on God's part for us to reject Him and to try to take His place in the world we have been given. The abuse of this freedom causes heartbreak and heartache for both God and us. It causes us to lose many of the freedoms we had previously been given. It is only when we surrender that we can enjoy those freedoms once again.

Once we let go, a sense of trust is developed. Trust that God, Christ, a Higher Power outside of us, will take charge and work it out. It is this fundamental change that brings with it a switching from the negative to the positive that is difficult to understand and explain. John Keller, in his book, *Let Go; Let God*, says "There needs to be an internal desire or readiness to let go, to quit fighting, and to give in both within the conscious and unconscious, within the intellect, and within the guts of a person."[21]

Surrender does not come without a certain amount of anger and even sadness. It is sad to think of giving up control. It is sad to let ourselves be powerless. Sadness helps us have enough courage in order to admit and uncover that which is at the heart and core of life, and then surrender those things blocking our health, wholeness, and security.

Surrender in the spiritual journey, at least for Christians, is found in the experience and remembrance of Baptism. Surrender is a daily dying to the old self and rising to a new self in Christ. Each time Christians confess their sins there is surrender. Like everyone else, Christians experience pain, brokenness, and limitations, things they have no control over. In spite of all that, they turn them over to God; that is surrender. Surrender is that recognition that not only do people not want to control everything, but more importantly, they cannot. In

44

relations this means allowing those around them to be more themselves so that the individual can be more of himself or herself. It is finally giving in to the fact that others need to be treated as children of God just as they do. Surrender is a step of faith and an expression of trust. One may not know where or how but one does know who.

The ancient Christian's credo was three words "Jesus is Lord." What does that mean in life? For each person it takes shape in life in different ways. Those who have surrendered can truly say that they have a pretty good idea who they are. They will follow the lead that Jesus has set. They will find ways to allow Jesus to be Lord over every area of life. Nothing remains untouched. They learn that whatever happens they can entrust themselves, their past, present, and future to His care and keeping.

In speaking before an AA convention Father Martin said, "My past is discharged, my present is secured and all other things being equal, my future is assured." Surrendering is one of the greatest acts of faith, allowing a person to say, "Thy will be done, not mine," and know that it will be OK.

Chapter 5

Step Three: Conversion

Whenever one speaks of conversion, what almost automatically comes to mind is the great apostle Paul. His conversion on the Damascus Road was so complete and so sudden that all other conversions are measured by his. He was filled with self-righteous anger, filled with self-justification, because he believed he maintained every legalist requirement of the law. He was critically defensive of all those who were different from him. He was a leader of his religious community. His actions and thinking are remarkably similar to the behavior and attitude of many alcoholics. But then came the dramatic conversion. His sight and speech were affected. From that point on he saw and spoke a different language. He became a different man, which is biblically attested to by the change of his name from Saul the Pharisee to Paul the Apostle. Although people generally think that Paul's conversion was instantaneous and complete, he spent seven years in the wilderness trying to fully understand what that meant even to him.

Within the Christian church there have been great revivals that have occurred at certain points in the church's life which have emphasized the necessity of a conversion experience. There are any number of denominations that have emphasized the need to have some sort of personal conversion experience. Other groups have avoided the subject completely. Those who have gone through a conversion speak of the gift of tongues, a wonderful sense of joy, an intense experience of the presence of the Holy Spirit, the urge for others to share in the same experience. Their world is different. They are different. There is a real "before" and "after" picture. Before the world was rotten, people were rotten, their situation was rotten, they themselves were rotten. But now everything is beautiful. There are no problems too big, there is no situation so bad, there is no relationship too far gone that they cannot be redeemed by Jesus and me. After the conversion experience there is a glow or enthusiasm, a positiveness.

Those on the outside are more than a little skeptical of the "new person." They wonder how long this will last before the "old person" comes back. Is this for real or are they just faking it to get out of some sort of problem they were facing? Since nothing like this has ever happened to me, they are sure that right behind that smiling face and peaceful look, that there is a lying, conniving, manipulator.

Both within the church and outside of the church there are skeptics and critics who have noted and kept track of all the negative aspects of the Pentecostal conversion experience. They have suggested that those who are attracted to such groups and experiences are people whose lives are awry, lonely, alienated, and insecure. Somehow there is a real attraction to have those needs met by going through this conversion. They have criticized the experience altogether. Those who have little or no experience with people who have gone through a conversion feel it does more harm than good. They argue that conversions cause more questions than they answer. Some of H. Tiebout's early writings are directed this way.

Right or wrong, good or bad, the conversion experience is not an end in itself. It is an invitation to a deeper search for the spiritual center and the response in life and values that evolve. It has both psychological and spiritual dimensions that can dramatically change the personality of an individual. Following the psychological model Tiebout says:

As I see it, conversion is a psychological event in which there is a major shift in personality manifestation. Whereas, before the patient was swayed by a set of predominantly hostile, negative attitudes, after the conversion process, the patient is swayed by a set of predominantly positive, affirmative ones. This shift, which may happen instantaneously or over a period of time, is to be considered a purely psychological phenomenon which can be studied independently of the factors which may bring it about.[1]

Tiebout admits that he does not have the same qualifications or clarity when it comes to discussing the religious impact of conversion. But he does realize that even though religion has many times failed, there is a "faith element" that is a part of the constructive forces residing in every individual.[2] Conversion is, then, a vitally important and valid part of everyone's religious experience and an authentic part of the spiritual journey. For many, it is called a spiritual awakening.

It is this personality shift that makes this so vital, not just from a psychological standpoint, but for spiritual development as well. A man mentioned that he was ambivalent to religion and spirituality. During an AA meeting one night he confessed that the Sunday School teachers and ministers of his youth were probably all saying the same stuff that he now felt was so vital and important but that is not what he heard. Prior to conversion, in the alcoholic to a greater degree and all of us to a lesser degree, there is blocking of what is heard, what is seen and what is felt. That's called denial.

In the preconversion state, whether in an alcoholic or a non alcoholic, people have the feeling they can manage it all. They are in control. They don't need anyone or anything else. Even before AA began, a man named Rowland H, as a last resort, went to visit Carl Jung in Switzerland for help from his alcoholism. The only hope Jung saw for this man was a "spiritual or religious experience, in short, a genuine conversion." Jung cautioned, however, "that while such experiences had sometimes brought recovery, they were still relatively rare."[3]

There is no way to accurately describe every conversion experience. Each is different, because each person is different. There is no getting around it. Perhaps the problem with the Pentecostal is that they try to replicate each conversion in exactly the same way. It is like running up and down the Damascus road, waiting for conversion to happen just like that of Paul. Any other revelation other than a blinding light will not do. As much as we try to avoid it, there is no spirituality without conversion. This was tough for a rationalist like Bill W to accept. "Conversion, the third facet of the core AA ideas, was a term avoided. Yet the profound reality of the concept was inescapable: 'bottom' clearly implied that there was something else 'higher.' "[4] But it is no less difficult for enlightened Lutherans. It is probably the reason that so many Lutheran Pastors look to the Epistle or the Old Testament lessons to find a sermon text on the day that the Gospel text is John's encounter between Jesus and Nicodemus. Being born again for many is not a part of Lutheran experience or theology.

Conversion is an inner change. It is a taking of the negative and the negatives of life and transforming them into positives. Conversion in the simplest sense is a changing from one thing to another. In a sense, every change of heart, change of attitude, change of awareness, from something negative to something positive is a conversion experience.

Henry Tiebout listed eight personality patterns of an alcoholic that describe the preconversion state of the individual.

1. Tense and depressed;
2. Aggressive, or at least quietly stubborn;
3. Oppressed with a sense of inferiority, while at the same time secretly harboring feelings of superior worth;
4. Perfectionistic and rigidly idealistic;
5. Weighed down by an overpowering sense of loneliness and isolation;
6. Egocentric and all that implies in a way of a basically self-centered orientation;
7. Defiant, either consciously or unconsciously;

8. Walled off and dwelling, to a large extent, in a world apart from others.[5]

Tiebout goes on to explain how each of these statements have been confirmed by interviews and counseling that he has done with clients. Each of the eight items is similar to what he experienced working with a number of alcoholics. The personality changes are so dramatic and so apparent that the person obviously went through a conversion.

In an interview with a woman who had come to a tremendous change in her life, he asked her to write a list of words that described the before and after of her conversion:

I Felt	**I Feel**	
unstable	at peace	
tense	safe	
nervous	composed	*I have learned*
afraid	relaxed	
guilty	contented	*the meaning of*
ashamed	thankful	
pushed	cleansed	*humility and*
incapable	sane	
uncertain	receptive	*meditation.*
unworthy	prayerful	

These issues are all basically spiritual issues. Too often people have tried to impose a medical model; the right prescription, the right medicine, or the psychiatric insight with the right therapy and right drugs. Depression, negative self image, self esteem, self righteousness (whether self or other directed) loneliness, isolation, pride, separation(s) prevent and inhibit spiritual growth and development. The lists from Tiebout sound like stories heard from AA members. There are biblical stories that mesh with each of these. This would describe the preconversion state of Paul. That is probably very close to the preconversion state of us all. As Tiebout says: "I am convinced, moreover, conversion from negative attitudes to positive ones is a phenomenon far more frequent than I personally ever realized."[6] A woman from an ACOA meeting said that conversion for her was like a "flipping." Something inside of her flipped and suddenly the world changed. A man in AA said he had had hundreds of conversions in his spiritual journey. Another woman described her conversion as a seven year single event in which she was in and out of treatment a number of times. There were times when she didn't know which way she'd end up. A friend said his conversion began when he become aware of the fact that he had another drunk in him, but he was scared he didn't have another recovery left in him.

Sometimes, people get the impression that once a conversion experience takes hold, it is instantaneous and almost effortless. Yesterday was like this; today everything is different. For Paul it didn't happen that way. After the Damascus road experience he went out into the desert for seven years to figure out what that meant. Whenever he describes his spiritual journey he talks about a great passion and tremendous effort. It is as if it is an ongoing struggle against his natural will. Conversion is a both/and process. It is both complete and it is continuing. That is how a person can mark the day he/she accepted Christ into his or her life, and it is how the alcoholic marks the time of his/her sobriety. And yet in reality one is converting every day to Christ, "a daily dying to the old self and a rising to newness in Christ." In the same way, there is an emphasis in the stages of sobriety.

Conversion can best be seen as one looks back and retraces the journey, and then, to see what that all has meant. Certainly, many can pinpoint a starting point in a flash of light, a loud voice, a felt presence, a bottoming out experience, a point in time. But more often than not it was out of the depth of despair, loneliness and self-centeredness that a still small voice broke through. It was out of the depths that persons somehow realized, for whatever reason, in whatever way, that their lives were unmanageable. The control and power they thought they had is only a myth, a lie, a deception that they tried to pass off on themselves and others. The admission of the un-manageableness of life provides a release that made things look new.

Most conversions are not rapid. They take time. Walls take time to tear down, barriers to feeling and trusting do not just automatically drop out of the picture. The process of letting go of the isolation and the re-establishment of lines of communication to the outer world, especially when there has been a lot of hurt along the way, is a gradual one. It is giving up of what M. Scott Peck speaks of in, *The People of the Lie*, called "magical thinking." By that he means that we believe that we can control events by our thoughts alone. According to the Christian model, Peck says;

> *Humanity (and perhaps the entire universe) is locked in a titanic struggle between the forces of good and evil, between God and the devil. The battleground of this struggle is the individual human soul. The entire meaning of human life revolves around the battle.*[7]

Those who have experienced a conversion experience, a transformation of the inner world, find that the outer circumstances may stay the same. People may be as flawed and inconsistent as before. They themselves may have just as many character defects, and may have to let go little by little. Situations may still be exactly the same as before, hardships and turbulence may exist as before. Without a doubt preconversion people have tried in every way imaginable to get the world to conform to their inner world. There is no deliverance from the stresses and hardships of the world. They somehow always will be there. There will be times when the person is angry at God. There will be times when God does not answer. Something will forever be a thorn in the flesh.

When there is surrender, and people realize that they are no longer God, they develop an awareness of a higher power. One's own personal power to control has gotten the person into the state they are presently in. Conversion comes when they listen to the voice of God.

When there is a change in attitude, there can be a change in personality. Conversion readies people for the next step.

What does this have to say to those whose lives seem to be going along okay, to those who consider their lives okay? The spiritual journey begins with a crisis. There is an awareness that something is wrong. It may be inside. It may be between persons. It may be a crisis in faith. The problem with all those who refuse to move through conversion is that they see no real reason to move through conversion is that they see no real reason to let go. They still try to maintain control. They believe they can have our power and retain their thinking, not change one thing about their attitude, and still be spiritual.

That is not the case. David experienced a conversion when he penned the 51st Psalm. "Create in me a clean heart Oh God, and renew a right spirit within me." When Paul speaks of "dying to sin and rising to newness of Christ," that is a conversion. Isn't the dichotomy between the old Adam and the new Adam much the same thing? When Paul speaks of putting off certain attitudes and putting on others, that is conversion.

The real heart of the matter is that if people are open to a spiritual conversion God will probably be wanting to change some of the things that they hold on to most dearly. People have areas in their hearts that are marked off-limits. Conversions most affect those attitudes and values that people hold about themselves and that they cling to most strongly. Perhaps here as in no other step one sees the difference between the religious and the spiritual person. The religious, the non-alcoholics alike, need conversion just as much, and it is just as urgent and lifesaving and lifegiving for them both.

Chapter 6

Step Four:
Emptiness

I called a friend shortly after I heard that his father had died. In the course of the conversation, he said that without his father around he felt so empty. He and his dad were very close. They had a special relationship which seemed to fill them both in many ways. Now his death left my friend empty of love, of companionship, and with an irreplaceable relationship.

On Easter morning the disciples and the women went to the tomb. The stone was rolled back, and the guards were gone. What should they think? How should they feel? The stone rolled back revealed only the darkness of the cave. The women stood for a moment. They began to wonder if this was a trick. Was it a scheme? Was it some sort of criminal act? Slowly, ever so slowly, they entered the cave. As their eyes adjusted to the darkness, they saw that the body which had been laid there two days earlier was no longer present. The linens that had wrapped the body of Jesus were all neatly folded, leaving no trace of what might have occurred in that room. Their eyes searched every inch of the cave, looking for a clue, or for an idea of what might have happened to the body of Jesus. Each of the disciples followed the same pattern. They would not just take the women's word, but they had to explore the emptiness of the tomb for themselves. They were not exactly sure what to make of the situation, but explore the emptiness they must.

The same is true for people today. The road to spirituality does not happen without one first exploring the emptiness. It is an existential dilemma. Most people will be unable to make the pilgrimage to a cave in Palestine. Instead, the exploration of the emptiness is the journey into the interior of life. It too, is scary. It is frightening to think what might be found or more importantly what might not be found. More often than most people would care to admit, they shy away from this journey. It always means pain and suffering. Since few people want to be a masochist, they try not to put themselves through the anticipation of that kind of pain.

Also, more often than people care to admit, they run straight away from emptiness. They look at themselves as optimists. They tell themselves the glass is always half filled, never half empty. They get involved in all kinds of activities because they are afraid in many ways of the emptiness associated with getting older. Their time is filled so that they do not have to be alone in the empty spaces.

In AA stories, each alcoholic, in his or her own way, has been drinking in large measure to fill the emptiness in their life. For many alcoholics that emptiness began as a child, when in his home with his family he was treated as a totally insignificant person. It is living with the consistent inconsistencies that create the feelings of insignificance. Somehow, some way, that innocent fragile self was degraded, demeaned, devalued, and that left the child empty. In an effort to fill that space, drinking or using resulted. "Somehow when I was drinking I didn't have to face the emptiness in life or the empty feelings that come from the way I was treated as a youth." For many AA people that self delusional grandiosity is the compensation for the emptiness of the inner self. Since there is no way to face it, the only thing to do is cover it up, or anesthetize one's self — temporarily denying these feelings.

The biblical challenge to fast is one of the ways to spirituality. It is a realization that I have come to in the last few years. Moderns have viewed fasting as archaic practice with ambivalent to negative associations. Contemporary Americans, especially middle class people have little if any personal experience with the Biblical mandate regarding fasting. When Jesus spoke of fasting, it was a positive thing. When he was in a crisis, he fasted; when he was struggling with a decision he fasted; when he ran up against demons so strong, so powerful, that it was going to take his all, he said the only thing that would help was prayer and fasting. Jesus used times of fasting to stop and evaluate what he needed to do, where he needed to go, what his mission was to be. In order to be focused and directed, he sought out times and places where he could fast in order to empty himself enough so that he could hear the divine answers. Fasting made the space within himself to really discover the new.

Modern people need to reevaluate the whole idea of fasting as a way of emptying themselves of routine and the ordinary and make room for the new. The point is that fasting makes space inside. It is pretty hard to hunger and thirst for anything without fasting. It is more difficult still to get new and different answers to life's existential questions, really different than the ones we have always gotten, until there is an intentional first step of emptying the self of all the predisposed and repetitious ways of normal thinking or doing.

Americans keep themselves at a constant level of fullness so that they do not have to experience the pain of an empty stomach. Meditation and contemplation happen best when people are empty. It is in the emptying process of meditation that a person can let go enough to allow something beyond our control to enter in. Only when bodies, minds, souls are empty can God move in to operate and take hold. It is out of emptiness that develops sensitivity which creates a new awareness of the mysterious and that which is beyond the ordinary. Spiritually, people can never address the real emptiness of their lives without first experiencing the physical emptiness which needs to precede this. But it takes work, it takes effort, it is always a painful process, no matter how many times a person has emptied himself or herself before. As M. Scott Peck has said, "Like any discipline, it can become easier if we make it a habit, as I have suggested Jesus did. But even if habitual, it is still painful. For emptiness always requires a negation of the self and the need to know, a sacrifice."[1] Maybe this is one of the reasons why so many alcoholics cannot refrain from drinking. They know if they quit, there is only emptiness that awaits them. For them, as terrible as things are now, it is scarier to face the emptiness of not drinking. Maybe this is the reason why so many religious types keep up their false fronts. The liturgy may be boring, the worship may be just as dead, faith may be seen only as an obligation, prayers as just so many words but they remain satisfied with what they have because these exterior rituals, are a better alternative than facing the total emptiness that awaits. It is no wonder there are so many nominal Christians, and that the world outside sees nothing different within the church than within society as a whole.

By the world's standards emptiness is something to avoid, something to deny, something to satiate, in whatever manner possible. No one would choose to be empty. Emptiness is something forced on a person. Empty experiences are painful. Empty living has no meaning or purpose. Emptiness is the natural progression from surrender. Like it or not, Americans are "control people." They like to control themselves, their environment, the people around them, and even God. Surrender means turning over control to a Higher Power. It is so hard to admit that that higher power is not "Me." Yet surrender is not one of those "once" for all experiences. It is daily, it is an ongoing process of life. To surrender means to empty the fortress of the inner self of all the arsenal of weapons of control that have been used to defend the self.

Emptiness is especially scary for those whose lives have been built around control. For example, if persons clean out their arsenals, who will then protect them? If they really empty themselves are they not opening themselves up to a whole host of experiences and feelings they might not be sure they are ready to handle? If they really get in touch with the emptiness around and within them, a whole new awareness will take place. For those in AA the emptiness has allowed them to permit space for their higher power. For the Christian the emptiness allows the presence of Christ to become a reality. Not that Christ was not a reality before, but without the emptiness there really is no awareness of the presence of God in their life. People must empty themselves of self-centered concerns and self-directed ways if there is to be further growth in spiritual understanding.

As M. Scott Peck points out in the chapter on emptiness in his book, *The Different Drummer*; "To survive, a community must repetitively stop whatever it is doing to ask how it is doing, to think about where the community needs to go, and to be empty to learn the answer."[2] Even though Peck is describing emptiness for the community, the process for the individual is the same. Peck's description has a lot to say to those in the church, in the community of faith, as well. The emptying process is not only a self directed process; it is more than an individual thing. It is the individual emptying himself or herself of all those things blocking that true relation with God as pertains to both the self and to the community in which one belongs.

Using Peck's insight of community survival, and applying it to an individual's spiritual survival, people must also stop repetitively what they are doing, and ask where they have been and where they are headed. Christians call that confession. Confession empties the person of false illusions. It opens people to a new awareness of their shortcomings and faults. It allows them to see those times and places where they have filled our lives with things that bring temporary satisfaction and self gratification. Maybe that is why through its history the Church has set aside Lent for this process of confession and self examination and considers it primary to spiritual restoration and growth. People may hate Lent because they hate the emphasis on confession and self examination. They are not ready to take the step of emptying the self of any of the thoughts, feelings, or attitudes which fill their lives. Those who miss the joy of the resurrection have probably not made time or effort to empty themselves of the sadness and sorrow within their lives.

This is one of the reasons those in AA have been able to learn so well this process of emptying self. They have experienced in a very real way, in a very painful way, the futility of filling their lives with false spirit. Before entering this step, people often say: "I am sick and tired of being sick and tired." In a very real way they have faced the existential dilemma of meaninglessness and lack of purpose. They have denied what was happening. They have tried to escape this step. They have tried to answer this all alone or with others who are drinking with them.

Emptiness makes room for the other and the totally Other in our lives. The AA experience should have taught people by now that the primary problem of the alcoholic is the inordinate place that the self plays in a person's life. As long as the self, the ego, the pride remain seated on the throne of power, there will be no room for God or any Higher Power. And as long as the self is in control there will be no room for one Higher Power to operate. It is an expression of narcissism.

In terms of the other, it is only out of one's own emptiness that they can identify and share in the emptiness of others. The other's pain and suffering will be of no consequence whatso-ever until one can enter their own emptiness and allow the other's emptiness to touch theirs. This is why in the past people have been so judgmental in relationship to the alcoholic. This is why there continues to be a controversy over defining alcoholism as a disease. This is why only moralistic pronouncements continue to be made toward the alcoholic down through the years. For those outside the AA family, there is fear of what they might discover if they truly risked entering their own emptiness. They must continue to maintain the upper hand. As long as a person feels superior, one can judge those whose pain and situation is more severe. Genuine emptiness puts everyone on the same level.

Several years ago our church, which has helped an inner city pantry, was asked if we would be willing to host a Christmas dinner for some of the street people whom the pantry serves. We saw this as a special opportunity. However, it was viewed by some as the great suburban church searching out and helping these poor, indigent, people. This would be a great benevolent effort on our part to share the spirit of Christianity. But something happened when the indigent first arrived. They all sat at their tables and we sat at ours. Then someone saw what was going on. People began to move, physically at first. There was an intermixing. It resulted in a breaking of the tension. Then the real movements happened. People were moved emotionally and spiritually. No longer were these others just street people. No longer were they the different ones. No longer were they the poor ones. They were more like us than different. They were people with feelings, people with joys, people who had the same things we did. The result: it changed us. It changed our outreach; it changed our attitudes. Sure, we still do most of the same things, and we are still involved with the pantry. But now we do these things for a different reason. We have shared the emptiness. The emptiness of our visitors allowed us to share not just in sympathy but now in empathy. We began to see, to feel, and to experience these people differently. We began to listen to them, to really listen in a new and open way. If we are to become empty, we must begin to listen not only with our ears, but more importantly, with our hearts and feelings. That listening can happen only when we take the time and effort to be silent. In AA, time is made at the beginning of each meeting just for silence. It is in that silence that the true reflections of the Spirit and the deepest contemplations of the heart can take place. Silence is something that most religious people give lip service to. When there is silence in the worship service, people get uncomfortable, and assume the pastor has lost his place and cannot remember what comes next.

The work and the movement of God come out of the silent places of the world. Both the birth and the resurrection of Jesus began in silence. When the world was silent, God acted. Elijah did not find God in the wind or the rain, but in a still small voice that spoke to him when he thought all was lost. God is waiting for people to be silent, so that He can come in to fill the emptiness with the presence of His Spirit.

M. Scott Peck describes the work of emptying the self as the place where the possibility and potential of real change and transformation in the personality and ultimately in all relationships. Peck equates the process of emptying oneself with Elizabeth Kubler-Ross' five stages of death. He says,

> *Kubler-Ross's stages of dying are also highly analogous to the stages of individual spiritual growth and to the stages of community development. For in every case we are talking about change. Emptiness, depression, and death are analogous because they are the concomitants of the bedrock we must reach if we are to effect change.*[3]

Spiritual growth requires a death, in fact it requires many deaths. These are deaths of the old self, the old ways of doing things, the Apostle Paul's phrase of the death of the old Adam, if there is to be a birth or a rebirth. There is no Easter without Good Friday, there is no resurrection without a death.

Whether approached from a psychological or a theological viewpoint the effect of emptiness is the same. Different terms may be used but the phenomenon is the same. Yes there are dangers, there are fears, there are risks in becoming empty. But affecting a deep and profound change within a person will never happen without first becoming empty. For it is in being empty that a person is led into new and uncharted territory. Traveling into the emptiness of one's life is always a process of discovery and trepidation. There is no way of knowing what the result or outcome will be. The only way that a person will dare to enter the emptiness is that there is a hope and promise that there is something better to be gained. It is here as perhaps no other place that a step of faith is required. Faith allows room for a Higher Power. Faith enters where reason and logic stay behind. But most of all faith comes from a personal willingness to enter the emptiness by silencing what has been and listening for what is new.

Chapter 7

Step Five:
Centering

When alcoholics talk about their past drinking, they tell about all kinds of ways home life revolved around the drinking. When things got bad they drank, when things were good they drank. When it was time to celebrate they drank. When others would hurt they drank. Almost anything said or done was an excuse or occasion to drink. For the alcoholic everything centered around the bottle.

A friend described to me how her husband's family all have problems with alcohol. They were visiting her husband's brother and his wife one evening. The conversation turned to restaurants and my friend was describing a restaurant she enjoyed. Her sister-in-law said, "Yes, we went there but we didn't like it. The food was good but it doesn't have the right atmosphere for us." As my friend later thought about this she realized that the right atmosphere meant this restaurant did not serve alcohol. And since it didn't, it was obvious it was a place her in-laws didn't like. Her brother and sister-in-law didn't go out to eat and have a drink with their meal, they went out to drink and if they had something to eat that was secondary.

For the alcoholic the focus is always on the next drink. They think about how, when and where they will drink again. It is that focus, that obsession, that has gotten life out of sync.

The same is true of the alcoholic family. The focus of their attention is on the alcoholic. Everything revolves around him and what he is or is not doing. They make plans according to the alcoholic. They make excuses because of the alcoholic. They refuse to do what they want to do for fear of how their alcoholic member will react. They are just as stuck, and just as sick, because their lives revolve around the patterns of drinking that the alcoholic member has established. When that happens life is out of whack, out of control and out of balance.

The movie *Karate Kid* that came out a couple of years ago was about a young boy, Daniel and the old Japanese mentor, Mr. M. Young Daniel wanted Mr. M. to teach him karate and he did. One of the most poignant scenes in the movie came when Mr. M. and Daniel were out in a boat. Mr. M. was fishing and Daniel was standing on the bow of the boat. It was hard to figure out why Daniel was standing there. Every so often, Mr. M. would rock the boat, quite unexpectedly. At first Daniel would fall into the water. But then gradually no matter when or how hard Mr. M. would rock the boat, Daniel remained standing on the bow. What Mr. M. was trying to teach Daniel was the art of balancing. Expertise in karate was not possible without first learning how to balance oneself. When the boat rocked, it was easy to fall in. But eventually Daniel learned how to balance himself. No matter what happened, he could remain standing. Before Daniel was taught any of the karate moves or maneuvers, his wise mentor Mr. M. taught him the importance of balancing. All else depended on that.

When I was working concrete construction years ago, part of our job was putting up foundations. We had to carry eight-foot by two-foot forms that were made out of three-quarter-inch plywood. They probably weighed close to seventy-five pounds. I can still remember the first day on the job, trying to carry the frames from the truck to the hole in the ground where the foundation was to be. Old George, who had been working as a laborer for 10 years, seemed to have no problem carrying the forms. But when I tried to pick up one of the forms, it was an absolute strain and struggle. I tried muscling the forms. I tried wrapping my arms around it to lift it. I tried dragging it. It must have been very funny to watch. Old George let me carry several of the forms my way. He saw how hard I was working, how little I was getting accomplished and he was delighted that a twenty-year-old college kid could be so dumb. Finally, when he could see that I had been beaten, he came over and said, "Do you want to know the secret to carrying the forms? They really aren't that heavy, you know. But the way you are trying to carry them is impossible, and we'll never get anything done." He said, "Reach down here and grab the form, center it on your shoulder and then lift it with your legs. The trick is to get the weight as close as you can and centered on your shoulders." I did and it was amazing. I could pick it up with ease. It was heavy but I could carry it anywhere. And what was amazing was that by centering the weight, I could keep carrying those forms without wearing myself out. Who would have thought that would have been the case?

It doesn't take much to get things off center, and therefore, out of balance. A slight shift of the weight from one point to another, can tilt the balance of the whole load. As long as the center is wrong, the balance will be wrong as well. But when the true center is found the balance is established as well.

Maybe that is why AA has been such a leader in this process. The founders of AA, as well as members of AA, discovered that their center was off and, therefore, life was out of balance as well. There are lots of people who have a compulsion that has driven their lives completely out of balance and off center. Whether you are talking about a workaholic, a spendaholic, or sexaholic, a pleasureaholic, it does not matter — they sought happiness in their compulsion. What once brought pleasure and a high, now brings only struggle and pain. That drives the addicted person further and further into the compulsion to find and experience that same pleasure.

Compulsion deifies the object of obsessions. That is why very early in the program Bill W and others realized that they not only had the wrong center of being, but in many cases they had no center at all from which to operate. That is what made this program a spiritual program. It was the search for a new center and, therefore, a new balance.

Basically the alcoholic struggles to come to terms with two things that claim their central attention — self and alcohol. They became twin centers that lead nowhere. Both claim god-like stature and allegiance. As alcohol takes more and more control of one's life, that life becomes more and more chaotic, both for the alcoholic and the people around him. As a result the person changes, relations change, attitudes and outlook change, values and what is valuable changes, and never for the better.

A novice painter had just completed a truly lovely landscape. Her family lavishly praised her work, but a wise uncle shook his head from side to side as he looked at the painting. "You don't like it?" asked the young artist. "Oh, I like it, all right, but it will not last," was his reply. "Your picture has two centers of interest — see, a large tree there, and a snow-capped mountain there. In time, people will be confused about the focus of your picture's subject, and even you will begin to dislike it. No work of art endures when there is more than one center of interest."

The scriptures are filled with reminders of life getting out of balance. Joshua tells the Israelites in Joshua 24, "Choose this day whom you are going to serve." Jesus tells the people, "You can't serve two masters, God and mammon. One will always have to take precedence over the other." "Where your treasure is there your heart will be also." Paul's letters to the early Christian churches are filled with admonitions and encouragement to choose the values and attitudes that reflect the will of God. Paul is always expressing the tension that the flesh holds over the spirit. Luther talks about holding two things in tension. For Luther, the two kingdoms, being simultaneously saint and sinner, law and gospel, old and new Adam, faith and works were all about the same thing — balance. Too much one way or the other disturbed the theology and the ethics of a people and the Church. Even though Luther ultimately wrote and believed that the Gospel had to predominate over the law, and that the new Adam was stronger than the old Adam, and that the Kingdom of God was greater than the all of the kingdoms of the world, nevertheless the tensions of the world did not go away. Armed with the scriptures, Luther's greatest achievement was to insist that God's side, God's works, God's presence was this strong new balance that could counteract the powerful grip that sin, death and the devil had on the person and the world.

It is so easy to get off center. The pulls and pushes of life are great. What makes them even worse is that they are often subtle and hidden. At what point did the young man become an alcoholic? What drink was the one at which point the man lost control? When did the little innocent child go from being open and receptive to being troublesome and unmanageable? When did the young person give up on the institutional church and become an agnostic and/or a cynic?

These are processes that go on and on and there is no point at which we say they have suddenly changed. Change occurs slowly, daily. Perhaps people just do not pick up on the signs.

God is the center of the universe, and the closer people get to the center the closer they are to God. When the ancients thought of the world in three tiers, God and heaven were just above the sky, beyond the stars that illuminate the sky at night. But increased knowledge of the universe brought a change in locating God. Heaven was less defined as a place and more defined as a true relationship. All that out-thereness was exchanged for the in-hereness. If heaven is a place where one is in total communion with God, then it would seem, the closer one gets to the true center, the closer one is to God.

One of the dominant characteristics of alcoholics is that they are people pleasers. They want to be all things to all people. Because they have such a desperate need to be liked they will behave, think or say anything. They will even take on the personality that they think others want from them. Since their world of reference is the people around them, they try to be all things to all people.

One young woman described her sister as a chameleon. Her sister has adapted the same ability as the chameleon to change as her surroundings change. Neurosis at its base is simply a conflict between what a person is and what they believe they are supposed to be. In psychological terms, schizophrenics could be defined as people who have lost their center and act this out in life. They struggle desperately to find that center. What is worse is that they often become involved in therapy with psychiatrists and therapists who have no center either. Therefore, progress is delusional and generally short lived.

Some business people say they have gotten sick and tired of living a schizophrenic existence. In the business world they are called to act, say and do things one way. That way is often contrary to personal beliefs and values. Yet, because they need their job, they continue. But in their family life, they are called to be something different again. They try to impose values and standards on their children that are in direct opposition to what they do at work. They are completely different again in their treatment and actions toward neighbors and people in the community. It is no wonder that people are so confused and troubled.

Centering our life on a Higher Power — for the Christian it is Jesus Christ — restores a consistency and constancy that the world so desperately needs. Whether in choices, decisions, options, alternatives, or the pushes and pulls, people need a center to return to, to check if their choices and thoughts are consistent with what they say and believe. It is from that same center that they return to the world to be and do. They can act not as the world and others call them to be but as God calls them to be. It is not without a price nor will it be without pain. It is what sent Jesus to the Cross. What attracted throngs to Him was the fact that He was the most centered individual who ever lived. But it is also what repelled people as well. Both friends and foes could not dissuade Him from the mission and purpose for which He was sent. The identification of Jesus with His father was so close and so complete that nothing was done without consultation with Him. But even Jesus needed times to get recentered. With all the demands and the pressures that Jesus faced, there were times when he needed to get away and be alone. Before He made any major decisions in the face of temptations, and as He moved in and among people, He took time out for reflections — quiet and personal conversations with God. He was centered and used those opportunities of prayer to become recentered especially when He felt that there was a good possibility of being moved off center.

People in AA bring up the word God many times in the normal course of their conversation. As they talk about what is happening, they will often refer to their higher power. The same kind of free flowing testimonial is just not there in most religious folks, at least, not Lutherans. The same is true in terms of meditation. Alcoholics know instinctively that they need quiet times and meetings on a regular basis. There is nothing that will interrupt that priority. If and when things are going bad they seek additional meetings to re-establish that balance and centeredness. One man said, ''I need to go to enough meetings, so that I want to.'' By this he meant that he knew that he needed to go to meetings regularly enough despite how he felt, in order to get to the point where he wanted to go. Another man was having real problems with anger. He would not just get angry, he would rage. That rage would set him back in his recovery and get him so far off center that it would take days or even longer to get back to where he was. One of his therapists who understood the concept of centering and what an important step it is in health, wholeness, and spirituality, told him that whenever he felt this coming on, whenever he knew something is going to happen that is going to throw him off center, whenever he came across someone who might disrupt his balance, he should take a little mini-quiet time to recenter and move on. He told him he may find that he needed ten or even twenty quiet times a day in order to find the center.

As Melody Beattie said in *Codependent No More*;

> *Much of the recovery is finding and maintaining balance in all areas of our lives. We need to watch the scales so they do not tip to far to either side as we measure our responsibilities to ourselves and to others. We need to balance our emotional needs with our physical, mental, and spiritual needs. We need to balance giving and receiving; we need to find the dividing line between letting go and doing our part. We need to find a balance between solving problems and learning to live with unsolved problems. Much of our anguish comes from having to live with the grief of unsolved problems, and having things not go the way we hoped and expected. We need to find a balance between letting go of our expectations and remembering we are important, valuable people who deserve to lead decent lives.*[1]

Centeredness does not just happen. It takes work. It is part of the spiritual journey. It will come only through prayer, reflection and quiet time. The closer one comes to the center the closer one will come to God. It is that spiritual communion with God that will set the direction in life, will guide persons in relationships with others, will shape the attitude(s) people hold, and will bring them the self-esteem and integrity that are missing without it.

No further progress can be made until one is centered in God.

Chapter 8

Step Six: Vulnerability

Dennis and Lynn were in my office one afternoon for marriage counseling. As we talked about what was happening in their marriage, it became apparent that they were keeping certain things about themselves from each other. There were deep thoughts that were locked in their past. Anger and defensiveness permeated the conversation. Lynn, who was normally quite outgoing and laughed easily, was quite explosive. Anger was right below the surface of every word she spoke. Their relationship was marred because of the times her anger got out of control. As we began to explore the anger, she talked about having a father who was demanding, strict and volatile himself. All her brothers and sisters had been victimized as children by her dad's strictness and uncompromising nature. Yelling and screaming were the norm in her childhood home. No one could do anything right. Every move, every word, every feeling was consistently and systematically criticized and belittled by their father. Her mom's passive acceptance of dad's actions and anger and her inability to step in and protect any of the children were regarded as her collusion with him.

As we talked about the anger she felt because of her father's treatment of her, Lynn opened up and told about several experiences she had as a child. Apparently her dad's violent anger and strict discipline were very real and very painful for her even twenty years later. These were events from her childhood she had kept secret from her husband and also herself. They were painful. She cried as she told about the details of the events. Her husband sat there and listened as she told about herself and her past that she had never shared with him before.

When asked how she could share these deeply personal feelings now and not before, she said it was because she had begun to realize that Dennis filled the role of her father in many ways. He, too, was strict. He, too, was demanding. He, too, was critical of her. Their marriage had become almost a father/daughter relationship in many ways. Whenever they slipped into those roles, Lynn would become that victimized child again. It had now brought their marriage to the brink of divorce. Then she told us that the main reason she could share this was because she felt safe in here. She did not feel safe at home. She did not feel safe with Dennis.

That night they got into a fight. As things heated up, and as the fight became a win/lose situation, Dennis pulled out some of the big artillery in his arsenal. Now he had a new weapon that had never been tried before and instinctively he knew it's capability and effectiveness. He used the information that he had heard in the counseling session that afternoon. Then he leveled her. It ended the fight, and also ended their communication for the rest of the week. As the smoke cleared, Lynn was again put into the painful situation that had grown so familiar to her as a child.

The next week in the counseling session, Lynn was uncharacteristically silent. She was obviously in her own thoughts and own world. Little happened in the opening minutes. Responses were a polite yes or no. Her husband began to talk about stuff that was not very important near the surface. I turned to Lynn, and asked what was going on with her. She burst out crying and said "I'm never going to say anything in here again. I thought this was a safe place, that what was said here was OK. But I found out differently. I can't share anything important here or anywhere. It is way too painful. It always gets thrown back in my face." Then she told me what had happened. And then she concluded by saying that every-time she let herself become vulnerable, she got killed.

Vulnerability is defined as being open to be wounded or injured; being open to attack; being sensitive to criticisms, temptation, and influence.

One of the many things that people learn early and learn well in childhood, is how vulnerable they can be. Children are born with an innate openness. They are open to love and security and protection. They are sensitive to the world around them. Even before they are able to verbalize they understand how safe and secure their world is. Children are vulnerable in every way to the care and nurture they receive from their parents. When their vulnerability is rewarded with nurture, acceptance, and loving care, they experience the world as trust-worthy and consider themselves to be important and worth-while. However, when their vulnerability opens them to a hostile environment, when those around them abuse them in any way, when they meet constant put downs and criticisms, there is a natural tendency to defend and protect themselves. It is a matter of survival.

Alice Miller has written several monumental classical works, including *For Your Own Good*[1] and *Thou Shalt Not Be Aware*,[2] in which she describes the evil pedagogy that children are exposed to. It is her thesis that people who experience vic-timization as children carry those wounds and scars into adult-hood, and into adult relationships. She has taken a worst case scenario of Adolf Hitler and of a convicted mass murderer and persuasively argued that one can explain and understand his behavior because of the severe abuse they received as a child. Biographies and stories of people show the effect of abuse of one sort or another on them as children. Depending on the type and severity of the abuse, depending on the child's in-dividual personality and temperament, depending on the child experiencing any dependability in the adults around them, chil-dren will reenact that pedagogy later in adult life and relation-ships. Those who have been exposed to this kind of pedagogy learn early and well not to be vulnerable. In their attempt to protect their inner child they split off part of their personality and take the pain that was inflicted upon them and turn it inward, so they become self destructive in one way or another. Or they turn it outward so that people and the world around them become victims of the rage and anger that they suffered as a child.

I have been counseling with several young men who describe themselves as survivors. All are in AA now. But in their teens and twenties these young men would just as soon punch somebody out as to look at them. They were always looking for a fight, and they generally got one. They talk about how tough they were. Though each has a different story, the common denominator is that they had each been hurt as a little boy. That little boy harbored lots of pain and lots of anger that was acted out in punching out others and self destructing in many ways.

In all of us there is an inner child of the past. John Bradshaw has done a lot of work in this area. In his recent book, *Homecoming: Championing Your Inner Child*,[3] Bradshaw gives a step by step account of how one can overcome the devastating experiences of childhood and how one can begin to love and accept the child within. The Bible says that a little child shall lead them. That has a messianic message, but there is also a message for every individual as well. It is the child in us that leads us and guides us in our adult living and relationships. That child will in large measure treat self and others the way s/he was treated in the formative and early years of self development. Those who have been hurt early and hurt often will have the hardest time taking this next step to spiritual growth and development.

The movie, *The Last Crusade*, presents an interesting study about vulnerability. That vulnerability is contrasted in the characters of Indiana and his father, Henry Jones. *The Last Crusade* is really a contemporary mythical story of the spiritual journey. It is really the spiritual quest of every man and every woman. The Joneses, along with several other characters, are in search of the Holy Grail. Each of the characters in the movie are searching for that grail for a different reason. Some are searching to destroy it, some are searching for their own self centered reasons, some are searching for the grail as an end in itself, as a prize to be won. But the real story is the father/son search. Henry is searching for the grail for illumination. Indiana is not sure what he is searching for.

Indiana Jones is the true American hero. Because he needs no one, he can fight armies and evil without assistance. He is the rugged individualist that Americans so desperately admire and seek to emulate. He is always in control. He is invincible and he is invulnerable. As a result, even after he has found the grail, saved his father, and his father has saved him, he still does not know what to answer when his father asks, "What did you find, Indy?"

Even though we know the character of Indiana Jones, we never know the person. He shows no vulnerability to enable himself to be known. When it comes to the question of what he found in the search for the grail there is no answer. Indiana Jones is really an enigma. He is a fictional man in a fictional world. Though you want him to win, there is no real idea of who he really is and what he is all about. There is no closeness to him. His relation with his father, girlfriends, strangers, and even the enemy are all about the same. The only thing you really know about him is that he hates rats and Nazis.

Jesus was a vulnerable person. The real strength of Jesus was in His vulnerability. He was vulnerable to human physical frailties and weaknesses. From His opening birth narrative to the closing words from the cross, Jesus is known to people and the world through His vulnerability. Because of His vulnerable nature He is open to the criticisms and the anger of the religious establishment. His vulnerability is evident in every encounter with the sick, the suffering, the sinners and the outcasts of society. In the garden of Gethsemene He willingly becomes vulnerable with God. In front of the Roman authorities He remains vulnerable to their accusations and questioning. When He was arrested and Peter came to His aid by cutting off the ear of one of the crowd, He heals the man's ear and asks, "Why did you come out here like this? Did you come out to get a criminal? You saw me in the temple, I have no weapons to protect myself. You could have done what you are doing under the cover of darkness at any time." He vulnerably submitted to the painful torture of the mocking, scourging, beatings and finally death on the cross. That is why the cross has been and continues to be the central symbol of the Christian faith. It is a symbol of ultimate vulnerability. It is the logical outcome of one who's life was characterized by complete vulnerability.

The kind of vulnerability that Jesus displayed in His living and His dying is contradictory to what the world has come to know and expect of its people. By cultural standards, the one whom we call Lord was born, lived and died in complete vulnerability. It is out of vulnerability that the strength and ultimate victory was won.

Yet there is no vulnerability without risk, just as there is no risk without being willing to be vulnerable. That is the way it has been and will always be.

In counseling with a young couple at church, both of whom had been wounded as children, I kept hearing that dilemma. He kept saying that he was "chopped meat." He often spoke of "putting himself out there," only to be wounded again. She kept saying they had no intimacy. He would refuse to make love. And when they did it was a mechanical thing that had no personal contact — only physical. She kept saying, "He is not there, even when we are together." They had a relationship that said whoever put themselves "out there" would be crucified by the other.

The idea of putting yourself "out there" is risky business. When one is vulnerable one opens oneself up to all kinds of possibilities — certainly failure, rejection, weakness, ridicule, being laughed at, and being wounded. Perhaps that is the core and the essence of Henri Nouwen's great insight of the wounded healer. There are no guarantees. "The greatest gift we can give each other is our own woundedness. The genuine healer has to be wounded. Only the wounded can heal."[4]

Those who have been hurt in life are looking for security and safety, for someone to take care of them. They seek, for good reason, to make themselves as invulnerable as possible. Yet when the defenses are set, there is no possibility of penetrating the defense system of that person. When one has been hurt deeply and often, they will shoot down everything, both the good and the bad, as a means of protection. AA people seem to have learned three things: don't talk, don't feel, don't trust. These three are the essence of vulnerability. As one distills the charges and countercharge to the common denominators, these three central issues appear and reappear over and over again. Talking, feeling, and trusting really put one at risk. It is the element of risk that makes vulnerability so difficult because there is always a chance of being wounded or even killed by those whose closeness and intimacy are so desperately sought after. But abundant life is dependent upon being open and therefore vulnerable.

> *There is no way that we can live a rich life unless we are willing to suffer repeatedly, experiencing depression and despair, fear and anxiety, grief and sadness, anger and the agony of forgiving, confusion and doubt, criticism and rejection. A life lacking these emotional upheavals will not only be useless to ourselves, it will be useless to others. We cannot heal without being willing to be hurt.*[5]

AA people are all very soft and sensitive people. These are folks who feel deeply and who have a tender soul. The problem is that all too often they get judged by what their actions are, they are condemned for crazy behavior, and they are labeled for being insensitive. The drinking, the drugging, the tough action, the anger, the projection, are all cover ups for the tender inside, the fragile self esteem, the incredible softness that was denied, condemned, or squashed in life's earliest experiences.

Certainly sensitivity is not an alcoholic phenomenon, nor is the defensive mechanism to cover things up. Being a pastor opens opportunities daily to enter into the pain and sensitive areas of people's lives. Pastors see those things at life's most critical points. There are plenty of opportunities for sharing in these same feelings on a daily basis. For example, we have a Bible study group of ten to twelve women that have been getting together for a number of years now. It has only been in the last year or so that the trust level has gotten high enough for them to share some of their weaknesses, family problems, questions, and heartaches with any degree of real honesty. Even though these women are very different from one another, and have been critical of one another in the past in outside settings and, even though they have not always liked each other all that much, it has been as they are vulnerable in that Bible group setting that the spirit of the group and their relationship with one another has changed. Now there is far greater understanding, more empathy for one another, and a more positive spirit that is growing.

Vulnerability calls for radical honesty. It is a willingness to expose the wounds and failures. After the resurrection Jesus appeared to the disciples and showed them his wounds. It was more than just proving to Thomas he had really died. Thomas' refusal to believe was really a refusal to be vulnerable. It was only as Jesus was vulnerable that Thomas would in turn be vulnerable enough to say "I believe."

> *I do not think that Jesus walked vulnerably among the outcasts and crippled of the world purely as a sacrificial act. To the contrary, I suspect he did so because he preferred their company. It is only among the overtly imperfect that we can find community and only among the overtly imperfect nation of the world that we can find peace. Our imperfections are among the few things we human beings all have in common.[6]*

Religious people always tell of how honesty is such a high value. Yet too often religious people are the people of the lie.

They pretend they have it together, mask hurts, stay in fixed roles, project and blame others for the same things they feel worse about themselves. Mutual honesty is about shared vulnerability which follows from acceptance of self and others as other than perfect. "It led in its turn to the shared honesty of mutual vulnerability that enabled at least a reaching toward ultimate reality and the touching of ultimate reality at least in human relationships."[7]

The reality is "we have all sinned and fallen short of the glory of God." (Romans 3:23) The reality is, "I do not do what I want to do, and those things I do not want to do are the very things I do." (Romans 7:15) The reality is "if we say we do not sin (are not broken) we deceive ourselves and the truth is not in us." (1 John 2:4)

In AA meetings they begin "Hi, my name is _____, and I'm an alcoholic." There are those who feel that this statement is demeaning and degrading. But what people fail to understand is the response of the group; "Hi, _____." It is in that simple response that there is recognition of vulnerability and acceptance. Those in the program have found great strength in both admission of weakness and the response of acceptance. It is here that the alcoholic could simply

be who he was and what he was, limited, and so able both to exult in the strengths that arose from his own weakness, and at the same time to be enriched by the different strengths that flowed from others who could not threaten because they shared the same weakness.[8]

That is nothing more or less than living out the great Scriptural paradox of strength in weakness. As one reveals brokenness, weaknesses, imperfections, shortcomings, there is a freeing strength that comes to life. Jesus taught it in the Beatitudes, he embodied it in relationships, he shared it in his tears with the grieving, he revealed it in his relations by allowing others to touch Him and by His willingness to enter their brokenness.

Jesus also spoke of being wise as serpents and innocent as doves. He knew there were times and places and people for whom and with whom vulnerability were not appropriate or healthy. Life is a process of learning and growing in knowing when and how and with whom I can be vulnerable. But He was always pushing people to open up and mirror the vulnerability that He embodied. The question people are asking today is, "Who are you?" and, "Who am I?" A number of years ago John Powell came out with a little book titled, *Why Am I Afraid To Tell You Who I Am?*[9] In it he spoke of this as the eternal question as long as people refuse for whatever reason to share their real selves with each other. In real ways people are enigmas to one another. And the only way to change that or to find oneself is to be vulnerable. Finding oneself and discovering who one is comes best in mutual honesty where one can share mutual vulnerability.

> *Mutual honesty about shared vulnerability followed from acceptance of self and others as other-than-perfect. It led in its turn to the shared honesty of mutual vulnerability that enabled at least a reaching toward ultimate reality and the touching of ultimate reality at least in human relationships.*[10]

One of the best compliments I have ever received came a year or so ago. It seemed at the time to be somewhat of a back-handed compliment. She said, "You know what I like best about your sermons is your willingness to be weak in the pulpit. Because when you share your struggles, imperfection, weaknesses, I have something I can identify with."

Carl Whitaker has the best perspective of all. He says the goal of therapy is a willingness to get in touch with his own craziness, and then share that craziness with people he is working with. He says,

> *It is critical for the therapist to recognize that craziness is where life is. Life is not social adaptation. Life is not the therapeutic hour. Life is not in any inter personal set. Life is in the expression of one's whole self; it is the fact*

of internalized individuation of personal, creative up-frontness. It is in the denial of slavery to rationality, slavery to conformity, the slavery of being culture-bound, time-bound, space-bound or anxiety bound.[11]

It is through the craziness that the real person to person contact is made. It is not only person to person, but also person to God contact as well. It is as people are vulnerable that they can begin to take their own personal inventory, and share who they really are with God, self, and one another.

Chapter 9

Step Seven: Forgiveness

Several years after the Civil War was over, Robert E. Lee was traveling through his beloved Virginia. A lady in Lexington, Virginia, recognized him as he was coming down the road. As in many areas of the south, several battles took place near this woman's home. She stopped Lee and said, "General, I want to show you what them damned Yankees have done to my home." She took him over to the front yard of her home and showed him the scarred remains of what once had evidently been a beautiful tree that had graced her yard. During the raid by the Federal troops most of the limbs had been shot off; there were holes where the bark had been stripped off. Thinking Lee would share her outrage, she waited expectantly for the General to comment.

Finally he said — "Cut it down, my dear Madam and FORGET IT."

What is it about people — good people, kind people, caring people, that keeps them from forgiving the wounds and injuries sustained in life?

How is it that a husband and wife can sit in church on Sunday and listen to a sermon on forgiveness? They can know what Jesus says about forgiveness, and affirm they believe that forgiving one another is important. Yet on Tuesday evening, when they come in for counseling, they can remember and repeat word for word every nasty thing said to each other for the past twenty years. Each in turn can drag up every hurt and injustice suffered throughout the duration of their marriage.

How is it that a young man or woman cannot shake free of the wounds of childhood? They were abused physically, emotionally, verbally. They were hurt, and hurt badly, and often. Now in adulthood, they carry that burden, that rage, that resentment, that hate, that has taken over their feelings and actions. No matter what they do or try to be, they cannot shake free of those wounds.

How is it that people get caught in an internal war? The body is the battle ground. The conflict wages on. There is no winning — only losing. The body, mind and spirit pay greatly for that war. Those who suffer from these internal wars end up with physical, emotional, and spiritual problems and cannot figure out why.

There is something in people which tends to overlook the one thing that can bring healing and wholeness and can restore sanity and peace. It is amazing how people can ignore the one thing that can get them unstuck so they can get on with their lives. That one thing is forgiveness. It is probably because forgiveness is the easiest and the hardest thing in the world to do. There is always an ongoing tension between the pain of life and forgiveness.

Forgiveness is the easiest thing to do because all one has to do is say, "Why not just forgive? All you need to do is forgive and forget and let life go on."

But there are times and reasons people do not want to forgive. Forgiving is so unjust. It goes against the idea of fairness. It feels very similar to the surrender process because it is a weakness of sorts. When people have been hurt it is not fair that they should be the one asked to forgive as well.

People do not want to forgive, because they do not like playing the role of victim. It is something they do not want to do. It means they have to change, and as much as they complain, they like it right here, in all of the pain and hurt.

People find it difficult to forgive because they do not want to let their defenses down again. They remember all too well the last time they did that and then still went on to get hurt. They don't want to take the chance that it will happen again.

Certainly, all of these reasons have some validity. None are wrong. Yet, the misunderstanding is found in the purpose and intention of forgiveness. From a religious standpoint, it is easy to get moralistic about why one needs to forgive, which only adds to the anger, the shame and guilt felt by those who are forgiving. "Genuine forgiveness does not deny anger, but faces it head on. If I can feel outrage at the injustice I have suffered, I can recognize the persecution as such, and can acknowledge my persecutor for what he or she has done, only then will forgiveness be open to me."[1] People can misunderstand forgiveness because they forget how powerful nonforgiving is. Not being able or willing to forgive someone can control one's thoughts, actions, desires, feelings, and relationships — not only with the one we cannot forgive but with all others, and not only for a short time but forever. "Whoever or whatever makes you feel guilty controls you."[2]

For a lot of people the problem is seeing where forgiveness begins and ends. Fundamental to the idea of forgiveness is who benefits from it. Forgiveness is not just for the person who has injured me, or whom I injured. If it stays on that level it remains only a matter of altruism, benevolence, tolerance, or excusing — none of which have much to do with true forgiveness. On that level it only deals with moralistic teachings that are sometimes associated with forgiveness. What brings about a change in attitude is coming to understand who the forgiveness is really for. Forgiveness is not just for the other person. First and foremost it is for the one who does the forgiving. What it does for the other person is not as important as what it does for the forgiver. To focus on the other person is to miss the point. Robert Ackerman, in his book, *Let Go and Grow*, has several chapters on making peace with the wounds of the past. In instance after instance, he counsels those living with deep wounds to confront all of those negative feelings head on. His main point is that one can only make peace with other people in life after one has first made peace with self.

To begin the process of forgiveness is to make a decision to forgive. At some point the declarative statement needs to be made, "I forgive you." For too long, the church has given the false impression that is it. Say the words "I forgive," and it is like waving a magic wand. Poof! it is gone. Gone is the anger and the hurt. Gone is the sense of injustice and guilt. It is like the mother who asks the injured child where it hurts, kisses it and makes it all better. Somehow, it is thought that like magic that kiss will stop the child's crying and allow the child to go back and play as if nothing happened.

But that is not it. The statement, "I forgive," is like the sign on the interstate in Nebraska that says "Chicago 400 miles." There is the good feeling that one is on the right road but one knows they still have got a long way to go before getting home.

Forgiveness is a process. It is a process of discovery. Carl Whitaker has said, "Nothing that is worth knowing can be taught. It has to be learned. It has to be discovered by each of us. The process of learning . . . is something you must struggle for in order to evolve more and more of who you are."[3] That applies to forgiveness so well. It cannot be taught, it can only be learned or not learned in the process of living. There are different stages in this learning process with different people all at the same time. There is no way to escape the process. People can only go through it and grow through it. As one forgives and becomes more forgiving the process becomes somewhat easier. Yet the road of forgiveness is always a difficult one to travel. No matter how many times one has traveled that road before, there are always new conditions, hazards, slow-downs, detours, and even stops that have to be made along the way.

Using theological language, forgiveness is a process of sanctification. Sanctification is a dynamic state of becoming. It is a growth in the spirit. It is becoming more of who a person is and an increasing awareness who Christ is and a growth in "Christ-likeness." To use the road illustration again, it is like being on the road, making progress, but never quite getting there. Yet, there is no frustration, because there is excitement in the journey and all the neat places that there are to see and the enjoyment of being enroute. It is like the old saying; "It's a progress not perfection." There is no perfection in the world, there is no perfection if forgiveness either. All one can do is make some progress in the journey of implementing forgiveness.

Perhaps it would be best to describe some things forgiveness is not and some things forgiveness is.

1. Forgiveness is not forgetting. One often hears the expression "forgive and forget." The Lee story at the beginning of this section would indicate the correlation between the two. Even when one forgives, one remembers too. Part of memory holds on to what ever injury was caused. With forgiveness that memory does not have to control and as time passes the memory does fade. But remember, only God can truly forget and say, "I remember your sin no more." Personal efforts at forgiveness are movements in this direction.

2. Forgiveness is not condoning what has happened, or saying that what has happened does not matter when, in fact, it does. Sometimes people figure if they forgive they can ignore a moral wrong which in effect devalues the person injured by that wrong. With or without forgiveness, right is still right and wrong is still wrong.

3. If forgiveness is not condemning, neither is it condescending. It is not something that is done by the person above to the person below. It is not a matter of rightness and your wrongness. The forgiver is not better than the one forgiven.

4. Forgiveness does not remove consequences. Even when people forgive there are often consequences that have to be paid. It is that forgiveness helps us live with those consequences in a far healthier and positive way.

5. Forgiveness is not just brushing aside what has been done, or the injury that has been caused. Forgiveness takes the problem seriously, and confronts it head on. When persons fail to forgive they are being far more evasive and are pretending no wrong exists.

6. Forgiveness is not all the same. Those who are in a special relationship like parent, spouse, child, are more difficult to forgive than others. Since these people interact on so many different levels, and are part of the family's ongoing history, there are more emotional losses and more old accounts to be settled. This makes forgiveness more complicated than ever thought possible.[4]

If, then, forgiveness is not any of the above, consider what it is.

1. Forgiveness is painful. There is no way around it. It is painful to live with the injury. But it is more painful to let go.

> *Our carescapes are nurseries of healing for the hurts we want to go away in relationships we want to keep. Forgiving is the healing art. It is the one way to make new beginnings at the painful point of where we are — not where we wish we were, but where we are, in pain, with the only person to whom we are coupled. The carescapes of promised love are watered with forgiveness.*[5]

2. Forgiveness is giving up power. Among the power forces of the world, forgiveness is at the top. Withholding forgiveness may derive a significant degree of power. It is a self protective use of power. Without it people can hold others in suspended animation for years. Yet with forgiveness, comes the Kingdom of Heaven.

3. Forgiveness is taking charge of life. It is a taking charge of the hurt that one has suffered. What the other has done or will do is not nearly as important as what the forgiver needs to do. Because few people want to be controlled by anger, resentment, stress, or negative thinking, the only release is found by forgiving. It is first something for the forgiver, then it is for one to be forgiven.

4. Forgiveness is a mourning process that brings healing for the wounds of the past. It is an experience of pain about the things that happened as they did. The past is over and done with and there is no way to change anything from the past.

A person often will be controlled by those events to the point that s/he keeps an ongoing open sore that continues to fester. When applied, forgiveness allows some of those old wounds to finally heal.

5. Forgiveness is work. It takes effort. It takes a conscious decision to say "I forgive." And then it takes work to make that decision stick.

6. Forgiveness is experienced as a form of grace. It is nothing that can be covered by rules and commandments. Rather it is a spontaneous result of freeing repressed hatred that has poisoned the soul.[6] It is entering into an empathetic relationship which is a disciplined, intuitive understanding of the other.

7. Forgiveness is peace. It brings serenity in the deepest sense of that term. The stressors in life, especially people, involve something that needs to be forgiven.

8. Forgiveness is always a three person affair. It involves the forgiver, the forgiven, and God. God is in every triangle. Forgiveness is not a human phenomenon. It is a divine action in the lives of human relations. It is a spiritual experience.

9. Forgiveness is moving on. There are so many people stuck in life, stuck in patterns of interacting, thinking or feeling, stuck in memories that they cannot let go of. Forgiveness allows people the ability to let go and move on.

Certainly these are not exclusive lists. Nor are they exhaustive. The reader could probably add other items to both lists. Yet they provide a working definition to help with that all important step.

It is hard to say that any one step is more important than the others. Forgiveness is possibly one of the most essential of all the steps. It is central to the scriptures, it was the purpose of the mission of Jesus, it has been one of the central facets of the Church's worship throughout the centuries. It was the part and parcel of the Oxford group from which AA had its earliest beginnings. Bill W and some of the other founders of the AA movement were profoundly influenced and affected by their association with the Oxford group. It was the

Oxford group that advocated the importance of working through the process of forgiveness. It is only through forgiveness and a vital awareness of its continued importance that spiritual growth can be furthered. In fact some of the other steps can be skirted or pushed aside for at least a time. It is impossible to do that with forgiveness. This is the step in the middle because the first six steps get one ready for this and the other five steps are the result of what is done here. It is pivotal. Forgiveness is where true spirituality stands or falls.

It is here that spirituality involves others and draws people into relations with others. Whatever happens on the interior of life needs to take expression in the day-to-day living with others in the world. There are those for whom spirituality is only a personal journey to the deepest, darkest recesses of the soul. It is a search for oneness with self and God. When spirituality is defined only as this type of personal piety then it becomes something akin to spiritual deception.

But spirituality is really a both/and process. Spirituality needs times of quiet, solitude, and meditation, and times of living, involvement with others and shared in community and fellowship. There are three primary sources for this forgiveness step. The first is AA and the stories of profound forgiveness of self and others that those in the program share. The second is three books on forgiveness that have recently been published. They are John Patton's *Is Human Forgiveness Possible?*,[7] Lewis Smedes' *Forgive and Forget*,[8] and Dr. Sidney B. and Suzanne Simon's *Forgiveness*.[9] Each of these works have renewed interest and understanding of this powerful part of spirituality. The last and most important, is the Bible which is the source and the guiding light leading us to a forgiving attitude.

Dr. Bob Smith, a co-founder of AA, described the 12 Step Program in six words — Steps 1-3, Trust God; — Steps 4-11 Clean House; — Step 12 — Help Others. In the AA's 12 Step Program, Steps four through eleven are really nothing more or nothing less than cleaning house by learning to apply forgiveness in life. The verbs in those eight steps are all action verbs about how forgiveness is embodied. Here is how they are stated: Step 4 — made a fearless moral inventory; Step 5 — admitted to God; Step 6 — ready to have God remove; Step 7 — humbly asked; Step 8 — made a list; Step 9 — make amends; Step 10 — continued to take personal inventory; Step 11 — sought the power to carry that out. Eight of the twelve steps are directly related to forgiveness. That has something important to say about how important it is to learn the art of forgiveness.

Alcohol/chemical dependency have a way of messing up life. It messes up finances, jobs, driving records, priorities, decisions, values, all sorts of things. But more importantly, it messes up relationships. It causes hurt everywhere. Alcoholic families look like they have been to the battle front, suffered a tremendous beating, untold casualties, and are now retreating. They look like the walking wounded, and they are.

During active use there were probably hundreds of times the user said s/he was sorry, and sought what was thought to be the forgiveness of family and friends. But nothing changed. In fact, everything was repeated and intensified. Forgiveness at that point did not change a thing, because nobody was changed. It is only after Steps one through three that a person in AA is equipped, humble enough, and aware enough, of where and how and to whom amends need to be made. Steps four through eleven the alcoholic is actively seeking to make amends, to take responsibility, and to do what can be done to bring forgiveness into a life changing focus.

Several years ago I led an Adult Forum on forgiveness in my congregation. Most of the time twelve to sixteen people attend that forum, but that series on forgiveness drew close to fifty for a six week study/discussion. Smedes' book called *Forgive and Forget*, was used. Smedes says that forgiveness is love's toughest work, and love's biggest risk. In it he describes a four stage process of forgiveness. There is the hurting stage — something has happened that has hurt someone. The hurt came in all shapes and sizes. The things that caused the most hurt came from people closest to one. It is like two porcupines. The closer they get the more apt they are to needle one another. People needle and hurt those closest to them. The second stage is hating. The hurt is internalized and it comes out again as resentment, especially if we do not do anything with it. People say they hate the sin, and love the sinner, but how often and easily do they slip into hating both. The hating stage can go on forever, pushing people further apart. More and more hate can be added on. Then comes the healing stage. It is a healing of self and then, hopefully, a healing of the relationship. But the first healing of oneself is not dependent on whether the relationship is ultimately healed. It is spiritual surgery inside your soul. With it comes new vision and new healing to the person who takes the risk to forgive. That risk brings an honest release of emotions and spirit. This is where a person makes a conscious effort to forgive. Forgiveness is really for the self. It heals the hurt and separation felt and experienced in one's heart. This may or may not bring the relationship together again. But this is not the reason to forgive. The fourth stage is the coming together. Certainly that is the desired outcome, that people become friends again, that they give the marriage another try, that they take what they've learned and improve the relationship. But even if people don't get to this step, forgiveness is a life changing force. As Smedes defines it: "Forgiveness is God's invention for coming to terms with a world in which, despite their best intention, people are unfair to each other and hurt each other deeply. He began by forgiving us. And he invites us all to forgive each other."[10]

Patton's book *Is Human Forgiveness Possible?* makes the valuable contribution of helping readers to see the one who has sinned against them as more like them than different from them. Often a person gets the notion that somehow the one who hurt them is some sort of malicious and vicious ogre. Too often they deal with their shame by searching for another's guilt.[11] And as long as they see this person as different from them, then no forgiveness is possible. As long as one uses the defenses of righteousness, blaming, perfectionism, rage, and resentment, forgiveness will always be illusive. It is only when one sees how much alike others are to them that they can truly forgive one another.

Dr. Sidney and Suzanne Simon's book titled, *Forgiveness*, takes seriously the profound wounds of the past, especially childhood wounds that one cannot seem to get over or get beyond. The "stuckness" causes so many emotional disturbances in oneself and not the one whom we are angry with or hurt by. The book is an important work in helping clarify the psychological understanding of forgiveness.

In a spiritualized programmatic way, AA has made forgiveness a rediscovered tool toward health and wholeness. The same is true of these latest authors on the subject of forgiveness. They help people understand the psychological workings that either prevent or promote forgiveness. They have given detailed analysis and practical and spiritualized psychology which is important and valuable.

Yet, they leave out the third arm of the triangle — the God side. God is the primary source and author of forgiveness. The closer one can get to the original primary source, the more original the work. Without God's forgiveness, human forgiveness is not possible. An appropriate title for God is "The God of The Second Chance." From the beginning, God has been forgiving and giving people second, third, fourth, infinite chances to restore, renew and rebridge the separation between Himself and His people, and between the people themselves. Much of the scriptures involve accounts of how and where, if and when people did or didn't forgive.

The history of Israel is nothing less than the ebb and flow of the Israelites in their relation with God. Sin is their separation from God and redemption is their return back to God. The Psalms, which are really conversations with God, are filled with admissions and requests for forgiveness. John, the precursor of Jesus, preached a baptism of repentance. Jesus and His ministry could be summarized as a mission of reconciliation and forgiveness. When He healed, he would say, "You are forgiven, take up your pallet and walk." To the adulteress he said, "Your sins are forgiven, go and sin no more." The parables repeat the same forgiveness theme. He established a meal of bread and wine for the forgiveness of sin. Even from the cross, the word of forgiveness is spoken.

Human nature wants to hold grudges, feel resentment, perpetuate the hurts. As a result people live in misery and make the world around them miserable as well. The divine nature of God lets go, or maybe a better word is forgoes, the hurt and anger and separations and instead replaces it with unconditional love and forgiveness. "The human task is to imitate God's action for us in our relation to other persons."[12]

The Bible says we love because God first loved us. We say and believe that it is God who both teaches and embodies love in such a way that people can understand and share that love. It is the experience of God's unconditional love that brings security, wholeness, and peace. The same is true of forgiveness. A person forgives because s/he has experienced forgiveness. Forgiveness is not conditional based on a person's willingness to forgive or not forgive. Rather forgiveness is a response to the forgiveness that is continually offered to the person. It is only when one can fully comprehend — maybe a better word would be experience — forgiveness in one's life and what it means to be forgiven can one begin to extend forgiveness in the relationships that need healing. John Patton calls it an experience of discovery of the power of God's healing spirit in a person's life.

> *Forgiving is not something that we have the power to do or are righteous in doing, but a description of the nature of our now-and-to-come kingdom relationship to God and to one another. Like God's kingdom, forgiveness is something that is discovered to be 'in the midst of us,' as a part of our neighbor-hood with one another.*[13]

The Lord's Prayer petition, "Forgive us our trespasses as we forgive those who trespass against us," has been interpreted to mean that a person's forgiveness is dependent on their willingness to forgive. That smacks of a human work, a conditional thing.

> *In the Lord's Prayer, then, 'to have debts forgiven is to be released from the burden of them.' Moreover, because our obedience to God is profoundly connected to our relationships with one another, the forgiveness petition can be understood 'both as a summons and as an invitation. It is a summons to the difficult task of releasing our claim to the right of judgment against each other ... And it is simultaneously an invitation to share in the greatest of God's gifts: the act of forgiving, of releasing others from their burden of guilt toward us.*[14]

There is a point when forgiveness is dependent on the willingness to forgive. But first and foremost one has to experience God's ever present word of love and forgiveness. When Jesus met the Samaritan woman at the well, he told her all about her past history. She was accepted, forgiven, changed. When all the townspeople came out to stone her, which they legally had a right to do according to Jewish law, He didn't get into a long drawn out discussion about why this woman was worthy of forgiveness. He just said, "He who is without sin, let him cast the first stone." What happened was that the people discovered something about themselves, that they were more like her than different from her. That is where true forgiveness lies. People need to be willing to be living in a relationship where they willingly get that honest. Individuals need to give up their pretenses of having it all together. It is only when an individual is secure in living in that relation that s/he can give up the denial of having been hurt, and their role in hurting others, and say, "Lord have mercy on me."

The step of forgiveness is forever a difficult one. It is work, hard work. There are no expert forgivers. The costliness of forgiveness is rooted in the preciousness of persons, not principles. It is a step that needs to be reviewed. Yet, it is the step that makes all others up to now make sense and it is the step that makes the future steps in spiritual growth possible. As Lewis Smedes concludes his book,

> *If you are trying to forgive; even if you manage forgiving in fits and starts, if you forgive today, hate again tomorrow, and have to forgive again the day after, you are a forgiver. Most of us are amateurs, bungling duffers sometimes. So what? In this game nobody is an expert. We are all beginners.*[15]

Chapter 10

Step Eight:
Present Presence

Often when one speaks to someone s/he gets the feeling the other person is not there. Oh sure, they are there in body, they are participating in the conversation, but somehow they are not there in spirit. There are times when people do that to others and even to themselves. People are so concerned with what is going on inside of them, or what they have got to do or what they want to say, that there is no way they can be really present with or for others or even for themselves.

It is hard to be honest, that honest with oneself and others. The alcoholic lives in a deceptive world. But don't we all? Somehow if people know the real me, they will not accept or like me any more. So we end up playing games.

There is the story of a young car salesman. That young man had been on a cruise with a high powered stock broker who was his superior, at least in a financial way. The stockbroker and the car salesman hit it off during the trip. As the trip was ending, the stockbroker said, "Listen, let me give you one piece of advice that has really helped me. When people come into your showroom, give them your undivided attention. Listen, really listen to them. Some might be there for five minutes, some for maybe an hour, but for whatever time they are there, be with them. Be present for them and with them. If you do that, I don't care what else you do or say,

I guarantee you will be a tremendous salesman because very few know how to do that."

Not only in sales, but in every personal relationship people have a hard time "being present." People are dishonest in their relationships more often than they are aware of or even care to admit, even with those nearest and dearest to them. Parents find themselves in another world when their children are speaking to them. They have something to say that is really important to them. They can hardly contain their excitement and yet the parent is hundreds of miles away from where their son/daughter is. Spouses play the game as well. Once married, spouses are many times heard to lament that their spouse is far different than they thought when they were dating. It is not that the spouse has changed, rather it is the dating process that is a massive delusional game that two people play. It doesn't take a husband long to not only tune out what his wife is saying but also, to remove himself from the constant talking, by unconsciously taking himself out of the picture. The wife may say, "I don't know how I could have been so blind to the fact that his drinking was causing so much trouble." Sexually, there are times when one wonders if the other partner is really there. Carl Whitaker says it as if a penis and vagina are taking a trip without taking any people along. In his book, *Midnight Musings of a Family Therapist*, he talks about family problems as being political problems that need to be solved. No longer is the therapist concerned with the Freudian issue of transference. Family relations, interactions, secrets all have to be understood before making any progress in helping. When dealing with families, Dr. Whitaker says, "You have to solve the political problem, and the first thing you need to know about the political problem is that nobody talks the truth. Nobody has any interest in saying what is really going on."[1]

Watch body movement/body conversation sometimes. People many times are long gone from a conversation before they finish talking. Studies have been done, indicating that people give signals that they are leaving, i.e., looking at their watch, looking around, stepping back, stepping forward, staring vacantly, which are all indications the person is no longer there. Their bodily movements are communicating one thing and their words are speaking something else. Generally it is the bodily movements that are closer to the truth.

Oftentimes, when I am trying to teach Confirmation students who would probably just as soon be anywhere else in the world, I use the tactic that seems to have more or less success — sometimes. What I say is, "This is going to be real important, and it will probably be difficult for you to understand. That's not your problem, it is my problem. What I need from you students is to stay with me." Stay with me means to focus on what I am trying to teach, follow the line of logic or reasoning, do not let the distractions get between you and me, and what I am trying to share.

It is hard to get people to be present. Not even Jesus could get the kind of present presence from those he was closest to. The night in which Jesus was betrayed His closest diciples could not stay with Him. He went out to the garden of Gethsemene to pray. He told his disciples, "Wait, be a present support. Stay with me." After each time of prayer, Jesus returned to His disciples, only to find them sleeping. "Could you not watch with me one hour?" is the question of Jesus. The answer is an obvious "No," and the events that follow — the fleeing of the disciples, the denial of Peter, and the way Jesus has to face the Roman Jewish crowd alone — give a stark reminder of the inability of the disciples to be with Jesus.

The eighth step in this spirituality is called present presence. The reversal of these two words is equally true. Presence present and present presence are qualities of those who practice deep spirituality. For whatever reason, the emphasis seems to be on the first word. The PRESENT presence means imminent closeness, now. PRESENCE present means there is an "I am with you" assurance.

People who have a hard time living in the present also have a hard time being in the presence, and vice versa. In order to live in the present presence there needs to be a massive reorganization project. Carl Whitaker calls this an existential shift. "... the challenge we all struggle with endlessly is that most of us live a fragmented life: we are either preoccupied with the horrors and the glories of the past, or we are preoccupied with the horrors and the glories of the future. We don't live; we just use our left brains to endlessly think about living."[2] All of the steps prior to this really need this one in order to take hold. It is impossible to really move in spiritual growth until this step at least begins to be worked on in conjunction with the others. The problem for most people is anxiety, which is the process of trying to live out of the future and/or depression which is the inability to come to terms with the past. Again Whitaker makes an astute observation of psychotherapy which is equally, if not more, true for spirituality. "I deduce, therefore, that the essential objective of all psychotherapy is to get rid of the past, good and bad, and the future, good and bad, and to just be."[3]

Some families have a hard time with this. Enmeshed families get so wrapped in what is happening to the others in the family that they become afraid to live in the present because it is too intimidating. This especially affects the children. "These children come out of their families with great guilt and anxiety, and what is guilt but a state of living in the past? Anxiety then is a state of living in the future, and there is no energy for the present."[4]

For many people it is the past that keeps them locked up and prevents them from living in the present. Something has happened at some point in life. Usually it is something that happened in childhood. Whatever it was, it has left an emotional scar. Jenna is a prime example. Jenna is twenty-seven years old. She has been living with her parents for the last five years. She is about one hundred pounds overweight and cannot get out of the house. Having grown up with an alcoholic father, Jenna bears many of the scars of having lived within that alcoholic system. As the oldest child she was given the responsibility of having to care for the family. As soon as she was of age she ran away and got married to an abusive alcoholic drifter. The marriage only lasted a little over a year. When the marriage broke up, so did she. She was hospitalized with mental problems and depression. Most thought it was because of the marriage. Her mother, a devoted and faithful church member, asked if I would visit Jenna. When I talked with her, I had my collar on. Right away I could tell the anger and the rage she felt were more than just surface deep. Trying to get me into an argument or vent her rage, she told me how she didn't believe in God. God had let her down all her life. As we talked it was apparent that my defenses about God or any reassurances that God was present only fueled the fire. God had let her down. God had taken the only significant people in her life away from her. Apparently when Jenna was eight to ten years old three significant others had died. A grandmother, an aunt and a cousin, all of whom she depended on and looked to for security and safety because of her crazy homelife, were suddenly taken from her life. Today she lives with unresolved grief of the past. She tries to control her environment by running the show at home. She has become the surrogate mother for her sister's baby and refuses to go out or let anyone else take care of the little girl. So the cycle continues. The history of the family system will not allow her to go on.

From the research and writings of Elizabeth Kubler-Ross and Ernest Becker, there is a greater understanding and appreciation of how powerful unresolved grief can be in an individual and a family. Children with behavior problems and poor grades, desire to stay in the "safety" of their home and room, withdraw from significant others, and live in a fantasy world. It is all a part of the inability to leave the past.

The same is true of others with turbulent family histories. Sometimes the past is so painful that it is either blocked out entirely or it is a secret so painful no one must know. The secret is kept even from the self.

For years Renee had been depressed. In fact people avoided her because of her depressive personality. She and others were convinced that most of it was caused by her first husband's many affairs. Not only that, Renee had become worse after her son committed suicide. Whatever it was, Renee seldom smiled. She really carried the burdens of the world on her shoulders. What came as a breakthrough for her was to find out that when she was six to eight years old, her uncle had sexually and physically abused her. By talking with her therapist, this hidden part of the past came to light. It didn't make her feel good to know she had been abused. But on another level it was like someone opened the door to happiness and ok-ness. After the discovery she began smiling, and the melancholy outlook disappeared. She had a new outlook on life and living.

Joan had also been victimized by her past. She had become a cocaine addict — always maintaining a happy facade. When you met Joan you saw a vivacious, bubbly, outgoing woman. But just below the surface was a woman filled with anger and resentment. Her anger was always a trigger for her cocaine use. Most of the time she would get real angry at her husband and his family. Her father died when she was sixteen and two years later her mother mysteriously died. She did not know the cause of death or anything else about her mom. None of the aunts and uncles would tell her about her mom. Her grandmother, whom she was very close to, would not speak about her mom. To make a long story short, this pattern went on for nearly ten years. Joan's abuse had cost her most of her father's inheritance, a marriage, and put her young son and unborn child in jeopardy. Finally she went into treatment. It was a first step. Yet when she got out she went back to using again only in a far more clever way. When she was readmitted she began to look at her past. There was something still missing. When her grandmother died, several of her aunts started talking to her about her mom, who had committed suicide. She learned of the manic-depression her mother lived with and the prescription drug addiction that her mom carried on for years. Joan has experienced a new lease on life, her program work has soared, she has a new attitude, and she has opened up lines of communication to family members that were severed for years.

For whatever reason, family secrets can hide the past and for years keep an individual and probably the whole system from moving into the present.

Most people are well aware of how guilt can keep them out of the present. Lutherans are experts on guilt. Things done or left undone can keep them forever focused on a past event that they feel guilty about. Guilt has a traveling companion close by called shame. Gershen Kaufman has done a considerable amount of work on shame. It has given tremendous insight on what and how shame affects not only what people do, and how they relate, but also their self image. Shame creates such a bad self image and low self esteem that no amount of present success or accomplishments can really provide the freedom to move on with life. People live as if time had never moved on.

The past has a lot to do with how people view the future. Because of the hurt and pain of the past, the future is always frightening. The main worry is now "what is going to happen to me?" Right now I have two grandmothers. Both are afraid of the future but in different ways. One grandmother is 99, and living with the constant fear of dying. She has had many minor strokes, several of which almost took her life. But she keeps coming back because she is so afraid of dying. She goes to church daily in the nursing home. She lives with the fear that she is not good enough, that somehow God does not want her. She vacillates between wishing she were dead and wondering why she is still alive. She clings on to life so desperately that nothing short of a full blown heart attack will take her.

My other grandmother has projected her fear of death into the family. Five years before my grandfather died, she told him everyday that he was going to die. Finally she got her wish. He gave up and died. Now she worries about who is going to

103

take care of her. For nearly the entire forty years of my memory this grandmother would walk my brother and me through the house, and tell us, "When I die you will have this, I want you to have that. But you'll need to take care of me." She lives with the constant fear that she will be abandoned. She uses things, money, the will, as a way to manipulate people to assure her that there will be someone there for her.

For nearly thirty years now Americans have lived with the constant threat of nuclear annihilation. Middle-aged Americans can think back to grade school days and the nuclear time clock that was being set and reset, always within ten minutes of midnight. That had a dramatic effect. That has had a powerful effect on our childrens' consciousness as well. And as Americans move into the '90s, the ecological annihilation of the earth may soon replace the nuclear threat as the number one concern for the collective conscious.

Ultimately it is the fear of death, and the denial of death, that really causes people to be unable to live in the present.[5] America is a death denying culture that looks at death as not only an unwelcome intrusion, but also as a failure on the part of human beings.[6] When the past is so painful, and the future so frightening, the present becomes unfit for living. It becomes like the great icy tundra, unable to support any life forms.

The children's tale of the ant and the grasshopper helps in understanding the past, present, and the future. The industrious ants worked all summer fulfilling the Protestant work ethic. Around them hopped the grasshopper who lived for the moment, paying no attention to the ants' warnings, and ignoring the change in the weather. For him it was eat, drink, and be merry and fiddle away each day. When the winds changed, and the blast of cold came from the north and brought the first snow, the grasshopper appeared at the door of the ants and looked in. The grasshopper lived in the present but for him and all his spiritual descendants there was and is no regard for the future or the past. Therefore, there was nothing to learn from, and nothing more than the moment to look forward to or get ready for.

True spirituality releases people from the past and assures them who is in ultimate control of the future, so they can really begin living in the present in new and different ways. Too often people have grown up with, or developed myths about what they can or cannot do about the past or future. More often than not, people develop this hopeless resignation of the past, and believe that there is nothing they can do, "What's done is done." People also believe this godlike overadequate myth about what can be done about the future, either as a "Que sera sera" (what will be will be), or "I can control everything and everybody" attitude. Somewhere in between is the balance, the key for taking this eighth step. Solidly rooted spirituality gets rid of the depression of the past and the foreboding anxiety of the future. Carl Whitaker says, "If you study the few grownup people in the world who have managed to make an existential shift to the present, you will find that the most dramatic aspect about them is their personhood — that is, their presence."[7]

In AA they talk about "one day at a time." The experiences of the alcoholic founders was that the past was often filled with so much remorse, guilt, and shame that there was no possibility of present living. They also discovered that the alcoholic was obsessed about the future. Drinking again was such a preeminent fear that it often pushed them back into alcoholic patterns. The alcoholic also worried about what effect the change in drinking might now have on affected family members. "What's going to happen to my family now, is she going to leave me?" And so the "one day at a time" principle became the watchword. "All I know is that with God's help I won't drink today. Tomorrow will have to wait. I can't tell you if I'll be sober tomorrow because I have no control over tomorrow. Tomorrow will take care of itself. It is today I have and today I am concerned about and today that I have control over."

The "one day at a time" theme, the importance of today is a central scriptural theme. What AA has used and emphasized are essential yet often neglected themes of the scriptures.

The scriptures certainly are aware of the importance of the past and history. God is a God of Abraham, Isaac, and Jacob. God is the one who has acted and been involved in the history of humankind. The mighty acts of God were the times in the history of Israel when God's presence and intervention had influenced the people, the course of events and ultimately, the course of history. The signs, seals, rituals and meals, were all important aspects of God's presence in the past. In fact all the covenants were reminders of God's promise to do in the future what God had promised in the past.

Throughout the Old Testament people learned and had to relearn to depend on God's present presence. Out in the wilderness God provided the manna for forty years. Each morning it was there in ample supply for the day, no more, no less. There was no way to horde or store any up for the next day. What God gave was sufficient for the day.

In the Psalms people struggled with the absence of God. "Where are you God? How long must I suffer, Oh God? How can I go on?" are all questions and cries of the Psalmists. As they lay their questions and anxieties before God, there is ultimately a reassurance of God's continual daily presence, "Thou art with me." There is a presentness that changes the outlook and there is a presence-ness that brings reassurance and comfort and hope that all will be OK.

In the New Testament that present presence is carried on even more strongly. There is an urgency to act today. What one does today is vital to your salvation. Jesus says to the penitent thief, "Today you will be with me in paradise." The man who builds the extra storage in anticipation of a bumper crop is called foolish because his soul will be called home that night. In Matthew 28, the final word of Jesus before the ascension, "I am with you always even to the ends of the earth," reaffirm that present presence.

In Romans 8, Paul says, "I am convinced that neither life or death nor the present or the future will separate me from the love of God in Christ Jesus."

Lutherans have always maintained the real presence of Christ at the sacrament of the altar. In, with, and under the forms of bread and wine, Jesus is really present. That real presence is a mystery. There is no explanation. It is a mystery and a doctrine that Lutherans and other Christians have battled over theologically for years. It is a doctrine that has separated them from other Christians. But the question is how many of them really live it? Christians need to take a closer look at this doctrine and begin living confident that the real presence of Christ is there with them always. In facing the problems and difficulties of life, Christian theology gives one of the greatest opportunities to practice the real present presence of God in daily life.

Living in the present presence of God is difficult, to say the least. It is not something that can be passed on to another. It is only something that can be experienced and witnessed. It takes a great deal of faith to let go and know that things will be OK. Yet, if Christians are to live in the present presence, they live with the confidence that the daily manna of faith, hope, and love will be there in sufficient quantities when needed.

God gives experiences that open the door of that kind of faith all the time. Jan tells the experience she had when her mother was hospitalized with a cerebral hemorrhage. The likelihood of her mother surviving was minimal. Each night when the family would get home from the hospital Jan would call the nurses station for one last report before going to bed. Then she would entrust the night to God's care and keeping. The sunrise each morning became a sign to her that this new day would be OK and that this was a promise from God. Each day, the new sunrise meant God would be there for her and with her for a new day. To this day, whenever Jan looks at a sunrise that promise and reminder of God's present presence returns.

God offers daily signs of His presence. Some are signs found in nature. A sunrise, a rainbow, a butterfly, spring flowers, a birth, all have been used in a religious sense to assure people of God's continued presence and promise for the future. But God communicates His presence even more dramatically through people. It is people who are touched by God's presence that can share that same presence with others. A friend once said to me, "If I am ever able to be present for you, I need a God who is going to be present for me." In the concluding chapter of his book, *Who Needs God?*, Harold Kushner seeks to find an answer to the question of why God is so hard to find. Kushner goes to the Psalms in search of a different proof of God. He makes a convincing argument that whenever the qualities that are generally associated with God such as love, honesty, generosity, courage, and altruism are a part of a person's life, God is present. He calls it "predicate theology."[8] He says, "Those are not statements about God; they are statements about love, truth, and befriending the poor, telling us that those are divine activities, moments in which God is present."[9] God works to make His presence known. People who are working to make those qualities and intentions known are really involved in a divine act, a manifestation of God's presence in human activity. God's presence lifts people's sights, develops sensitivity to the plight of human need, restores those who stumble and fall, renews the spirit when it has reached its limit, and points people to a future in which God's purpose will be realized. The present presence of God is lived in relationship to those both near and far. Kushner gives a dynamic definition of religion when he says, "Religion properly understood is not a series of beliefs about God. It is an inventory of moments in our lives, things we do and things that happen to us, in which the person whose eyes are open will be able to see God."[10] Developing a faith and trust in the present presence of God is always a difficult step. Confidence in that presence comes out of the depths and human experience. Those in AA have those experiences in abundance. That is why they are taking a continual inventory. It is an inventory of those moments of the where, how and through whom God is present for and with them. It is in that inventory that they come to realize what God has promised is, "I am with you." It is all anyone needs to face life with hope and courage, with security and confidence. It is God's present presence that is enough.

Chapter 11

Step Nine:
Restoring A Healthy Dependence

Family systems teach a new appreciation of how interdependent families really are. Systems thinking helps one see how each member of the family is related to the other members of the family in such a way that any change in one will mean a change in all. There is a homeostatic balance that is maintained in every family, even if it is an unhealthy one. But, the system resists the changes and puts lots of pressure on everyone.

Within AA and AlAnon circles, the new catch phrase has become "co-dependency." As Melody Beatie describes it:

> *Codependency is many things. It is a dependency on people — on their moods, behaviors, sickness or well-being, and their love. It is a paradoxical dependency. Codependents appear to be depended upon, but they are dependent. They look strong but feel helpless. They appear controlling but in reality are controlled themselves, sometimes by an illness such as alcoholism.*[1]

Though AA focuses on the disease, codependency is far broader than that, and affects many people in one form or another. John and Linda Friel argue that codependency is an integral part of our culture. "Just because you don't drink alcohol does not mean that you are free from addiction. You could have all of the traits of an addict — the denial, the discomfort with intimacy, the need for unreasonable power and control, the

111

inability to let go, the inner torment, the insecurity masked by grandiosity and so on — without being an alcoholic.''[2] Codependency is just one sign of an addictive society. This term has been defined countless ways by various people who have studied the phenomenon. John and Linda Friel define codependency the following way:

> *Codependency is a dysfunctional pattern of living which emerges from our family of origin as well as our culture, producing arrested identity development, and resulting in an over-reaction to things outside of us and an under-reaction to the things inside of us. Left untreated, it can deteriorate into an addiction.*[3]

It is this addictive way of relating to one another that is so destructive to relational and personal development. This addictive way of relating produces all sorts of symptoms within a person and between persons. The addictive process simultaneously keeps people together and apart. It is a condition where people live under an oppressive set of rules, rules that prevent the open expression and sharing of personal and interpersonal problems.[4] Salvador Minuchin has added a lot to family therapy by describing the transactional style of disengagement and enmeshment. When taken to an extreme these two polarities offer little if any possibility of individuation or autonomy.[5] There is no ability to come or go, only to get pulled in. It could be described as the Blackhole Family where everyone gets sucked in, and also as the Reversed Force Field Family where everyone gets pushed out. In neither one is there any freedom to come or go. Family members are afraid to come in because they will never be able to return again.

Codependents of any sort have real troubles with boundaries.

> *Family membership is determined by both external and internal boundaries. 'Boundary is a metaphor referring to an imaginary line that distinguishes between members and among systems.' Ordinarily, membership in a family*

depends on such external determinants as marriage, birth, or adoption. The internal boundaries of a family are often unspoken; we become aware of them only after we have crossed them. [6]

Therefore, codependents have no idea where they end and others begin. Boundaries let certain things in and keep others out. For a lot of people their boundaries are either too weak or to rigid.

It is our belief that the underlying reason that we can't see these healthy limits is that we are desperately afraid that we will be abandoned if we say 'No.' Fear of abandonment is the primary dynamic beneath most dependent and addictive behavior, in our estimation, and how we get this way has a lot to do with the other two types of boundaries we spoke of. [7]

There is no trust in these kind of families or individuals, because it is so confusing. Because they do not know their boundaries they look to others as reference points for how to think, feel, and act. They hand over control of choices to others. There is no internal reference point from which to operate. Their reactions are based on how others act — always trying desperately to get those around them to like them. In marriages this can create a pseudo intimacy by reinforcing a mutual dependency. Since neither partner can operate without the other an illusion of security is created. In *Women's Reality*, Anne Wilson Schaef calls this an addiction. Here is her description of the codependent woman.

The nonliberated woman is dependent, self-centered, externally referented, out of touch with her feelings, etc., just as the addict and the co-dependent are. She gets her identity completely from outside herself; she has no self-esteem or self-worth; she is isolated from her feeling; and she spends much of her time trying to figure out what others want so she can give it to them. She is lonely because she is estranged from herself. She is controlling

113

because she has no self and is so dependent upon others. Her entire life is devoted to her husband, and her children, and yet she is experienced by others as self-centered and controlling. The non-liberated woman and the co-dependent are the same person.[8]

Here is what she says about the man.

He spends much of his time doing what is called 'impression management' — trying to make others see him as he wants to be seen and believing that he can control their impressions. Because his point of reference is external, he too has lost his identity. The non-liberated man overworks, overdrinks, and overeats, pushing himself to an early death. He becomes a zombie, who moves through life and does not live it. His dishonesty with himself extends to his relationships, his business dealings, and his entire life. He exhibits the same characteristics as the chemically dependent person does and these characteristics are precisely the focus of the man's movement. They are dealing, in fact, with the same syndrome. The labels are different; the focus is different; the perspective is different; and it is the same systemic disease.[9]

In an effort to live up to other's expectations, standards and values, they get stuck, and cannot see that there are alternatives and choices for them. "In the family a balance between individuation and participation is necessary in order that people may learn how to live together separately."[10] Codependency is prevalent in families because it is as Anne Wilson Schaef says, "Tacitly and openly supported by the society in which we live."[11] It is far more widespread than in just the alcoholic family. It has been the identification of this addictive process that has been such a valuable contribution from AA. Anne Wilson Schaef gives her full agreement when she says, "I firmly believe that since most people in this society are trained into an addictive system and the addictive process, most people could benefit from working a 12 Step program, or something similar to it."[12]

114

Dependency is one of those things that touches people's lives in a myriad of ways. Not only in marriage and families does this exist, but government has become like a cosmic parent that has an unending store of resources and programs to take care of people. When the government takes care of people long enough and well enough, not necessarily in the right way, people come to expect that it will always be there with this cosmic breast from which people will never be weaned.

Dependency does not build trust, only fear — fear that someone will not be there for the other person, fear that the giver will take away what the other wants most, fear that the caretaker will not take care of the other any more. That kind of dependency gets perpetuated in homes, families, marriages, churches, and society as a whole. It is passed from generation to generation as the accepted way of ordering life. What happens is that neither the one taking care of or the one being taken care of has any trust in the other. Typically, in a family where this first takes root, the parent assumes absolute authority and domination and control over the children, demanding submission and obedience and creating a dependency. It is no wonder so much of this dependency and reaction to the dependency gets transferred to the relation to God. The one being taken care of is just waiting for the rug to be pulled out, for love to be withdrawn, for feelings to be denied, for help to be withheld in one way or another. The one who is doing the care giving is just waiting and watching for the dependent one to screw up, for him to need the care giver some more, for the care giver to move in and take charge and let the child know how bad, weak, or stupid s/he is. In reality it is a no win situation, because the dependee can always be more dependent than the caretaker.

Dependency and codependency are learned behavior. Codependency is an

unhealthy pattern of learned behavior, attitudes, and feelings that make life painful. It is a dependency on people

115

for things outside the self to the point of self-neglect and diminished self-identity. The important words here are 'learned' and 'pattern.' If co-dependency is a learned behavior, it can be un-learned by changing patterns. [13]

Here are a couple of examples. A man, aged sixty, has a daughter in her thirties. She is divorced and has one child aged five. He grew up in the depression, went into the service, came home and worked his way up to a very successful position in a utility company. His personality is such that he is very neat and clean. He is absolutely meticulous with his personal appearance, with tools, cars, home, and everything. Whatever he is, his daughter is the exact opposite. She has made a career of allowing — maybe a better word would be forcing — her father to taking care of her. When she got her divorce, her dad bought her a house in a very nice area. His idea was that this would provide a nice place for her and her daughter. Her job was to make the house payments. But it was not more than a month or two before she started missing payments. The maintenance of the house was being neglected as well. She lost job after job that her dad would get for her through his contacts. She was raising two hundred rats in the house and that drove him crazy. He would yell and scream at her. He will complain to anybody who will listen to him. He has had some physical problems that caused serious concern. Finally, he bought a town house and moved her in there. She is on welfare. But this place has been trashed as well. He says he would let her go out on the street if it were not for little Natalie. But if he kicked her out, his little granddaughter would be on the streets as well and he cannot bear to face that responsibility.

It is interesting that he has said he has prayed and prayed about this but to no avail. Therefore, there is no God. If there was a God he would have come in to take care of the situation.

Another example involves a young woman in her thirties, never married, with a ten-year-old son. She had been a member of the church for six years. During that time she had a

116

good job working in a warehouse, making about $25,000 a year. But surprisingly she was kicked out of several apartments for not paying her rent. Commonwealth Edison shut off her lights several times, and the phone was yanked out for non-payment. After that she lived here and there and bounced around. I was concerned for her welfare so I co-signed on a mobile home. But soon the place was trashed. She was always calling about this or that wrong. No matter what I did, how much I did, it was never enough. I got the feeling she was always one step ahead of my need to help. She liked it best when I was doing things or working on the trailer. She always needed something. She was always depressed. She was always having money problems. And rather than do something for herself she would wait for me to take care of her. No matter how long it took me she would wait longer. Her life could be miserable but that was just a part of the game. What happened was that I felt an increased resentment of her anytime she called. I found myself impatient with any of her needs. I finally sat down and wrote her a letter explaining that I was already happily married and had my own family to take care of. I could not handle two. I would be there for her when I could, but I realized that I was not helping her by being responsible for her life.

Two months later she moved back to Ohio. She is doing better, maybe not great, but better than she ever did in Chicago. As soon as I unhooked her codependency on me, she was free to do or go wherever she wanted.

I learned that there is an important difference between caring about someone and caring for them. When we do things for others that they need to do for themselves we are making ourselves indispensable and we are not helping them. By taking care of someone we are facilitating their continued unhealthy dependency. That's called enabling. And that is unhealthy for all concerned.

Carl Whitaker says that when people start talking about needs and getting their needs met, they are probably moving into a parent-child dependent relationship. There are some

117

pretty needy people who are just looking for a surrogate mother to fulfill their needs that were never met when they were children. People in the helping professions need to keep a constant vigil for dependency transference. Last summer, I received a birthday card from a woman whose father died of alcoholism and whose mother has been hospitalized for mental disorders. On the card it said "Happy Birthday, Dad." That gets pretty scary. Again to quote the Friel's: "Unhealthy dependency means that the attachment that we have to a substance, a job, a person, a pet, or whatever is getting in the way of our happiness and contentment."[14]

Spouses sometimes take turns in the parenting role with each other. Children, even adult children, can stay in a dependent state, ever at the call of their mom or dad. Then the reverse can take place and the children can assume the parenting role for their parents. As Carl Whitaker many times describes this type of family interaction as if they become grandparents to themselves and their other siblings.

Whatever surrogate role people assume does not fulfill the dependency needs of those they are trying to help. That kind of dependency will never bring happiness or the fulfillment for the one playing the role of parent or the role of child.

Dependency is a type of relationship — not a good one — but it is better than none.

Spirituality is a movement to the interior of life and a movement back into the interrelated relationships. At its best, these relations should be mutually satisfying, based on trust, strength of personality, respect, and a freedom of commitment. Healthy dependency has to be both. There is a search into the interior and an expression in the exterior of who or what is really trustworthy in this life. This is a difficult process, and it is complicated when a person has grown up in an alcoholic or other dysfunctional family.

> In a healthy family, children's needs for security, warmth,
> nurturance and guidance are met most of the time. These
> children enter adulthood with a sense of security and trust
> that is inside of themselves. In dysfunctional families,

these needs are not met enough or at all, and these children enter adulthood with a sense of incompleteness, mistrust and fear inside of themselves, along with a strong need for some kind of security outside of themselves.[15]

One of the women attending an AA meeting while I was writing this paper asked what I was writing. When I told her about healthy dependency, she said, "Don't forget to talk about detachment." To be sure detachment has a lot to do with dependency. Detachment means to pull away from whatever one is obsessed with, whether that be a chemical, a person, a thing, or whatever else. It is an important part of taking care of oneself. Detachment takes seriously that each person is responsible for him or herself and not everyone else and their problems. Self care is an attitude toward the self and one's life that says, "I am responsible for myself." "I am responsible for me, for every aspect of my life, and it is OK not to be responsible for everyone and everything else." Decisions, feeling, thoughts, and desires are all a part of each person's responsibility. This plays an important role in the type of spirituality a person has.

If one wants to know about how any of the pioneers in the field of personality development actually developed the theory of the personality that s/he did, great insights can be gained by paying attention to their childhood. For each of those leaders in the field of personality development, it was their own early child experiences that directed their later thinking, emphasis and approach to the person and personality. What is true in psychology is equally true in a person's theology. If one wants to know about what kind of God most people have, look at what kind of childhood they had. A person's God image or even lack of it comes from the earliest days on this earth. As infants, every person is totally dependent upon his/her mother to meet every physical need. But a need of a greater sort was being met as well. For it is in a mother's arms, that a person makes an essential spiritual discovery of whether this world is secure and trustworthy and whether someone is there that cares what happens. That is the basis for all spiritual life and growth. The Scriptures translates the experiences of this world that provide security and trust into people's relationship with God. "God dependency is an active process that replaces the dialogue of the codependent self with the very words of God. The words of God tell us about health and protection and safety and about our sacred self."[16]

How often do the Psalmists speak of God as the rock and refuge. Jesus talks about building a house on the rock. He tells us that though the mountains quake and the world around crumbles God cannot be moved. Jesus says, "I am the same yesterday today and forever." The same is true of trust and that which is trustworthy. God makes many promises to his people about the idea of living in a covenant relationship. "Lean not on your own understanding, trust God and trust also me." Those who come out of an alcoholic family have a tough time with this one. What is interesting is that we have had AA groups meeting in our church for nearly seven years. Some of the groups have grown to nearly eighty people. But until last year very few people would come to church. In the last six months about twenty or so of those AA people have started worshiping on a regular basis. Some are joining. It was not because they did not like the church and worship was not important, but it took a long time to build up the trust that this church did care about them and their presence.

Remember the game show, "Who Do You Trust?" There were several contestants who were lying and one was telling the truth. Since it was a game it was always fun trying to guess which one was telling the truth. Those who come from healthy families play this game. But the odds are stacked in their favor. There are a lot of people who tell and embody the truth, there are many folks in their life who are trustworthy. They can pick contestant number one and he is trustworthy, and they can pick number two and she is trustworthy as well. Oh, sure, there is always someone who is not trustworthy, but basically the world is good, people tell the truth, and significant others are trustworthy. Just the opposite is true of an alcoholic family. They play the same game, but the rules are changed. Because the family is enmeshed in the disease, most members of the family are untrustworthy and the trust is distorted. People can try contestant number two, number three, number four, or number twenty-one and they will all let them down. So what is learned and experienced is that no one, not even oneself, is trustworthy. The family members have experienced that as long as the disease is controlling relations between self and others and God all are deemed untrustworthy.

As an example, a woman of our congregation who had been married to an alcoholic for five years was supposed to drive to a friend's house for an AlAnon meeting. She said she would lead some others who would follow in their own cars. As she got close to her destination, she began to panic about which street to take even though she had been there many times before. She could not trust herself to make the right decision, so she finally pulled over to the side of the road and let someone else go first.

The other part of spiritual dependency is the need to know if there will be somebody there for the one who trusts. Healthy dependency stands or falls on the creditability of the one who is believed. Infants need someone to take care of their physical needs. Humans are dependent for a long period of time on parents to take care of their physical needs. Those who do not get those needs met suffer from physical abuse and all that entails. But more than that, people need to know if someone will be with them emotionally. Are they loved? Are they important? Are they worthwhile? That emotional "being with" has more to do with self esteem and ego strength than anything else. This correlates to the spiritual "being with." Scripturally and spiritually the promise and the affirmation is "I am with you." God went with the Israelites in their desert wandering. God was with the Israelites during their exile. God was with the Psalmists in their deepest sorrow and depression. In the New Testament, Jesus is named Emmanuel which means

"God is with us." As Jesus prepared His disciples for His departure he told them He would send the Holy Spirit, the Comforter, to be with them. When He ascended to Heaven He declared, "Lo, I am with you always." Paul's great affirmation of certainty in the Book of Romans says, "Nothing, nothing, can separate us from the love of God in Christ Jesus."

What this has to say about spiritual and emotional growth is that it is very important to know what God one is hooking self esteem with. As God is, so are you. As your God goes, so do you. As your God does, so will you.

That is why the Bible makes such a big deal about the God of Abraham, Isaac, and Jacob. It was so easy for even God's people to wander and follow other gods. Even though they had been saved and had many special revelations of God in their history, their history was filled with times and places when they worshiped false gods. That is why the Scripture writers refer to the God of Abraham, Isaac, and Jacob. Even though each of those three men had different experiences at different times with God, it was the same God who had called and led them all. The same is true of the contemporary spiritual world. There is a temptation to follow and worship other gods. Healthy spirituality and healthy dependency are seriously distorted when a god other than the God of Abraham, Isaac and Jacob is followed and trusted.

Several years ago we had a woman in our church who spoke of "God this and God that." God was always taking care of her and her family. She used God as if He was her personal bellboy. The ironic thing was that she had three breakdowns, her husband had two, and her son is a big time pusher and cocaine user. But everything is beautiful and wonderful because she has her God. Her God is no more or less than a reflection and extension of her own grandiose ego.

People who are very angry are probably covering up some deep seated hurt. The anger is a projection of that hurt because it is never allowed to be integrated into a part of the self. Therefore, as Alice Miller says,

He has the need to strike out at others only if he is
thoroughly unable to understand his rage, if he was not
permitted to become familiar with this feeling as a small
child, was never able to experience it as a part of himself
because such a thing was totally unthinkable in his sur-
roundings. [17]

Hurt has often been thought to be the lowest level in a person's life. An AA counselor told a group there is another level lower than the pain. That level is a person's self esteem. How could a person ever have a healthy self esteem if every present situation is nothing less than a re-experiencing of childhood fears of abandonment when s/he was dependent on a strict, distant, and unavailable father?[18] Alice Miller goes on to say, "The greatest cruelty that can be inflicted on children is to refuse to let them express their anger and suffering except at the risk of losing their parents' love and affection."[19]

Those who have a trust and dependence problem have probably hooked their self esteem to the wrong God, perhaps justifiably so, but the wrong God none the less.

AA proposed and indeed operated on the assumption that
this denial of dependence upon ultimate reality was at
root a denial of the reality of the spiritual. It was this
denial of the spiritual that AA found underlying all the
other denials so characteristic as to be pathognomonic
of alcoholism. [20]

That's why the first three steps of AA have to do with establishing the higher power. According to Lynne Bundeson, alcoholics were struggling with past experiences with God and looking for new practical definitions of God.[21] For the alcoholic, acceptance of the reality of a higher power is the only way back to wholeness and happiness. For Jews and Christians the first commandment is, "I am the Lord your God, you shall have no other God before me." The rest of the Scriptures is a clarification of what that God is like and the experiences of people who trust that God. It is the Scriptures that are the single most helpful book available on the recognition and the healing of dependency.[22]

There are no atheists because everyone has a god or gods. Those who claim they are atheists basically have decided to be their own higher power. People who have made gods of things, whether those things be money, cars, high tech toys, or big houses, are looking for exterior validation and compensation to determine self worth. Their creed is, "The one with the most toys wins." Ernest Kurtz says, "The First Step of the AA program pointed out to the alcoholic this frustrating irony. His refusal to accept dependence upon ultimate reality — the refusal implicit in the claim to inordinate control — has led to a perverted dependency upon the virtually unreal."[23] Those who are locked into alcohol/chemical dependency rely on an artificial center for their self esteem. When alcoholics are actively using or codependents continue in a relationship without any support, they have little or no self esteem. It is little wonder that denial is so strong as long as one feels bad about him/herself. It is not surprising that as a spiritual center takes hold and begins to redefine one in relation to the new higher power, one can give up the denial. "Symptoms of codependency in political language are called 'loss of boundaries,' 'safety,' 'protection,' 'information,' and 'rights.' The healing or management of codependency is pursued in religious terms: 'God,' 'Higher Power,' 'trust,' 'forgiveness,' and 'gratitude.' "[24]

The modern mind has always understood the essence of full maturity as being absolute and total independence. Modern culture advocates independence as a solution for the problem of dependency. What AA has done is given a modern twentieth century insight while also maintaining the ancient pietistic understanding and advocacy upon God. The remedy for alcoholism is not the elimination of dependency or codependency, but rather, the focusing on God as the proper object of dependence. The alcoholic has found the problem is not the dependence itself, but rather, the distortion of it. To be human is to be dependent. Immaturity is focusing on the wrong object of dependence, whether that be a bottle, a person, or a thing. There is an integrity of dependence if this dependence is on an ultimate, absolute higher power that is outside the control of human experience. AA stresses a dependence on other people, but that fellowship dependence is based first and foremost on the first step of absolute dependence on God. What AA has done has taken an often neglected biblical understanding of life and brought it into the twentieth century and made it applicable and understandable to the modern mind. Christians need to reintroduce this absolute and fundamental dependence upon God if they are to have any significant influence in guiding the community of faith in a relationship to God. Healthy dependence is living within the grace of God.

> *God dependency is based on the premise that God is all-good and all-powerful and that each individual is free, regardless of parents' addiction, to recognize, understand and put into practice that goodness and power for him/herself. A basic tenet of God dependency is that each individual, regardless of past or present circumstance, may turn to God and find help and freedom. This idea that each person has a direct and accountable relationship to God is still a radical thought in some circles. But its basis in Judeo-Christian thought is thousands of years old.* [25]

What prevents healthy dependence is the demanding human nature. All too often people make unreasonable demands upon themselves, others, or God. They live on the extremes. They either try to dominate those relationships by becoming so authoritarian and God-like, or they try to subordinate themselves to the point of allowing the relationship to control them and becoming over dependent upon them. It is only healthy, proper dependence upon God that allows people the freedom to live within limits. "Proper dependence was the only true independence. In the 'spiritual program' of AA proper dependence was first upon God. The more we become willing to depend upon a higher Power, the more independent we actually are."[26]

Perhaps that is why at AA meetings you hear people say, "Hi, my name is _____, and I am a gratefully recovering alcoholic." Wouldn't it be a surprise some morning at worship to hear people say, "Hi, my name is _____, and I'm a gratefully recovering sinner." Or, "Hi, my name is _____, and I'm a gratefully recovering Lutheran." Then the grace experience would truly be a "grace experience." People are attracted to the Lutheran church in part because of the theology of grace that is professed. At the same time they get turned off because it is often not lived out. To appreciate grace one has to have bottomed out at some point in life. That is why the best prayer, the first prayer, but hopefully not the only prayer, is "Help." When one asks for help, one is coming to terms with the fact that one is not in control of the situation and needs a power greater than oneself to turn to and turn things over to. They have started, or renewed, the path to God dependence. They stop feeling helpless for a moment with the understanding that there is probably something that can be done to get out of Hell. It is as one man told me, "I've been to the bottom and the bottom holds."

Healthy dependence is the hitching of one's self esteem to God's unconditional love. It is only unconditional love that has the power to transform one's life. As Paul says in Romans 5:8, "While we were yet sinners Christ died for us." That is unconditional love. It is a love in spite of rather than because of. Unconditional love is total acceptance of what one is right now. And who one is now may not be who one wants to be, but unconditional love accepts the person none-the-less. In fact, unconditional love will change that to "always-the-more." God's grace is "always the more" than people expect or deserve. The scriptural affirmation is that nothing can separate people from the love of God. God has a way of loving people always the more. This little poem describes the unconditional love of God.

126

God loves me so much
that I can love God so much
that I can love me so much
that I can love you so much
that I can love me so much.

It is in the acceptance of who we are, where we are, and how we are that we can begin to affect the kinds of changes that make a difference and that we can control. "Acceptance is the ultimate paradox: we cannot change who we are until we accept ourselves the way we are."[27]

When an AA meeting breaks up, people will often stop in to my office to visit and say hello. They talk about miracles they have experienced. I listen to them talk of their higher power or God moving them in this way or that. I hear of prayers offered up in almost a conversational matter. I listen as they tell me there are no coincidences, even though bad things happen to everyone. But there is an acknowledgement of the hand of God in the affairs and experiences of daily life. I listen as they share some new insight of trust or God's presence that they have gained from their readings in daily devotions. For me that is a powerful testimony of healthy dependence.

On Sunday morning in the narthex after worship I listen to church goers speak about what is happening in their lives. There is talk of football and cars, of school and children, of parties and the latest gossip. What's interesting is what is not spoken, more so than what is spoken. There is little or no talk about God or prayer or the presence of God. People talk about what they are doing, how they are getting along, how they are coping. There is no talk of devotions or Bible reading or even any of the personal disclosures that become real person-to-person contact. This is a powerful testimony as well.

This is the "Let go and let God" step. For it is only in trust that people can begin to let go of the things that they have for so long tried desperately to control, including God and others. It is living within limits. It is the humble recognition and admission that people are not God, never have been,

127

never will be, even though they have probably tried more times than will ever be known.

All people are well aware of things that they cannot control, like the economy, war, the forces of nature. This recognition and admission of lack of power over the forces of the world comes far easier than does admission of lack of control in one's personal world. There is a powerful myth that a person can have absolute control over oneself, one's destiny, and especially over others and how they feel and act and respond.

Americans live in an addictive society. It is addictive to not only alcohol and chemicals, but to success, the work to achieve that success, to sex and pleasure, to gambling and money. And what is true of addictive societies is that people really struggle and fight against God-dependent living. It goes against the individualistic self-reliant ethos. American heroes are those who beat the odds and succeed on their own. They say: "I do not need God; I can take care of myself. I have all the personal inner and outer resources to take care of whatever happens." People are too busy being successful to think about God. They don't want another being, let alone a distant and remote God, to tell them what to do, how to live, and where they might be invest themselves differently. They want to control their own future and their destiny.

A battle for control — that is what this is all about. Alcoholics are well aware of this control issue. It is what their disease is all about, especially on a spiritual level. It is why alcoholics are very personally and painfully aware of how demonic and destructive this control issue is. It is a continual struggle in sobriety to turn over controls to the higher power. They know painfully well what it means to trust others and get burned. Every alcoholic has a story to tell about when and how they have been taken advantage of and abused, and they have vowed unconsciously to never let that happen again. It is part of the reason that relationships were, and still are in many cases, so difficult. When you have been burned it is hard to go back even if the burner is off. That is partly the reason relations, meetings, and sponsorships are so important. It is a re-establishment of ties to healthier people who can be depended upon.

Alcohol dependency destroys the myth that one is in control. Those who have tried to control the dependency have found that their lives are really out of control.

> We must discover God for ourselves if we want to discover spiritual self reliance. We can discover God in a group or we can discover God in the silence of the Spirit wherever we are. But to discover the nature of God and our spiritual, sacred self we must silence the dialogue of our senses. We must stop arguing with ourselves on both sides of the fence. We must live up to our belief that we are isolated in shame and that we are damaged from youth and always missing the mark because we descended from Adam and Eve.[28]

It is not until they have been broken down, on their knees, that hope and life are re-established. Out of the brokenness there is a recognition of the need for God. When the Bible talks about being driven to God, the alcoholic immediately knows what it is speaking about while the non-alcoholic is bewildered. The alcoholic intuitively knows that without God, life is out of control. The paradox is that as control is relinquished to the higher power, more control than ever is gained.

That is not to say that there is nothing a person can control. There are lots of things one can control. Taking care of self, loving others, speaking well of others, learning to respond and not just react to certain people in certain situations and, to a large degree, personal happiness, attitudes and what is done today are just some of the things a person can control. People have more than enough to do just taking control of things like these. What needs to be let go of are others, what they say and think, how they feel and act. There needs to be a letting go of judgmental attitudes, anger, moralisms, and the desperate attempts to control God. All these lead to the delusion that one can control much more than s/he can. "Dependence on

God means the relinquishment of all forms of socially adaptive codependent behavior. It means relinquishing an addicted, codependent self in order to find one's own unique, healthy and sacred God-dependent, God-related, spiritual self."[29]

Healthy dependence allows the grace of God to knock a person to their knees. It has everything to do with humility. It begins at baptism. "To be baptized means at one and the same time to be chosen and named by God as a distinct individual and to be incorporated into a community that transcends all human particularity."[30] God's grace grants security, the strength to cope, and the wisdom to make positive decisions. There are things that impact people's lives that are beyond their control. The question is whether they can humble themselves in order to trust the God who is trustworthy and unfailing.

That is why the Serenity Prayer is such a powerful and yet humbling prayer. "God, grant me the serenity to accept the things I cannot change and to change the things I can and the wisdom to know the difference." Not just saying those words but really praying them and then applying them to daily life will go a long way toward promoting and guiding people into a new spiritual step of healthy reliance on the all encompassing love and grace of God.

Chapter 12

Step Ten: Tolerance

During the '50s and the early '60s, the Ed Sullivan Show was the main TV entertainment on Sunday nights. Sullivan's show was perhaps the most well known and the best of all the variety shows that filled the air waves. He had animal acts, jugglers, pop singers, opera stars, comedians, and new talent. There was a little something for everybody. In those days people would watch the entire show. They would sit through the parts that they did not care for, because they knew that there would be other parts that they really enjoyed coming later in the program. No one would think of turning the program off when the opera soprano was on in order to wait until the comedian came on. No one would turn the channel because they hated certain performers, and only tuned in to see the Beatles.

Variety shows are a thing of the past because people have become intolerant in their TV watching tastes. People today turn off or switch channels to get something they want. TV producers and sponsors are very sensitive to the viewing public's tastes and know they will only tune in to those things they like.

This is analogous to the spiritual journey. Lack of spirituality demands sameness. People cannot relate to those who are different than they are. In fact, difference is a real threat both to them and to what they believe.

The step of tolerance can only come after total surrender and acceptance. Those who are intolerant are more often than not trying to control the world around them. With surrender and acceptance comes an increase in tolerance of people and their idiosyncrasies and different ways of doing things. The spiritual person can make room for the variety of understandings and approaches and ways of expressing the ultimate center and higher power of life.

Religious people through the years have often come across as highly intolerant. Conflicts have resulted between Christians and Moslems, Christians and Jews, Moslems and Hindus, Jews and Moslems. Holy wars have been fought in the name of every religion. In the middle ages crusaders were instructed to stamp out the infidels. Inquisitions were held in order to bring people into the "right way" of thinking. The purpose was to conquer. They would pressure the conquered to believe in what the conquerors thought they should believe and act the way they thought they should act.

Beginning with the Puritans, many of the New England colonies were established because of religious persecution elsewhere. Later on in American history the Mormons were constantly on the run because of the intolerance in the communities where they settled. Much of American history itself has been shaped by the people moving to one section of the country or another in light of the way they were first treated in their previous home or area. In succession, the Catholics, the Jews, the Mormons, all were viewed as a threat to the dominant Protestant culture.

What is true on a grand scale in religion is also true on an interpersonal level. Between people there are crusades and holy wars. Interpersonal communication involves grand inquisitions and missionary conquests in the name of one's God. All of the great movements that tried to stamp out, change, convert others, started on a one-to-one level. Somehow people think they have a lock on truth. They believe they alone know the way life should be handled, what should be believed, and how it should be expressed. Therefore, they will do everything in their power to change others around them so others can be just like them.

Intolerance takes expression in any number of ways. Perhaps first and foremost, intolerance is expressed as judgmentalism. There is a desire to judge others, to play God over them, evaluate them as worthy or unworthy based on an individual definition of what is right, holy and acceptable. If that other person or group deviates from that just a little bit, they will be let known in no uncertain terms. They will face a pronouncement of judgment over them in order to bring them back into line.

Intolerance is a very "righteous stance" toward events and people in the world. Intolerant people cannot bend, or be flexible, or express spontaneity. Within marriage or family systems the structures or problems of the family often revolve around those things that the family is most intolerant about. Rules, roles, and family rituals that are deviated from cause the most pain and family members work hard to bring whoever deviated back into line.

Intolerance is expressed in fear. Fear of another's difference, fear of change in oneself, fear of losing control, fear of not being loved any more, are some of the fears that spark intolerant behavior in people. The closer another person touches those personal fears deep within, the stronger the reaction will be. The greater the fear in a person or group, the more they will try to control others around them.

Intolerance is expressed by treating the other as an object instead of a subject. As long as that person remains an object, they can be manipulated, directed, or controlled for whatever personal reason is seen to fit. When the other is seen as an object they can be treated as an "it." This is the way hate, prejudice, bigotry are perpetuated. They keep those who are feared or deemed inferior as far away as possible. It is impossible to put a human face on those people in those situations. They are pigeon-holed into categories. In relationships it doesn't matter what the other thinks, feels, or wants. What does matter is that they fit categorical definitions and expectations.

Intolerance is evident in people who cannot deal with their own personal feelings. This has been one of the areas where AA has shared some powerful insights. At a meeting that was focused on feeling, a man sat quietly at a table in the back. When it came his turn to speak, he said, "You know I've been thinking about all of this feeling stuff. I've had a tough time with feelings all my life." He went on, "You know I've been put down, told I was stupid, crazy and everything else. I used to cite all kinds of facts for why I wasn't an alcoholic. I used to get irate when other people didn't have their facts straight either." Then he concluded with the very poignant observation, "If a person can't deal with their feelings, they have to deal with facts, and those facts have to be perfect." It is no wonder that so many alcoholics are perfectionists. They have become perfectionistic in their efforts to escape their own feelings. This is especially true of their feeling of selfworth, acceptance, and tolerance of self and others.

Finally, people are generally intolerant of the qualities and the characteristics in others that they hate or cannot deal with in their own lives. People are scared of those things in others that they are really scared of in themselves. Check and see sometime what it is that people hate in their spouse, in their children, in their parents, in neighbors, friends. These will generally be the very things that they have within them that gives them the most difficulty. In counselling people tell me, "I can't stand this or that." Taken at face value, they appear very noble and right. However, if one scratches the surface a little bit, there will be a part of the self that they are very uncomfortable about. What happens in relations is that people project onto others what they are scared of or hate in themselves.

The misconception of tolerance is that if one becomes more tolerant, if one takes this step in your spiritual growth, then one will have to like everything that comes along. That's not true. Because a person practices tolerance doesn't mean that s/he will necessarily become like the one they are having a hard

134

time with. Nor, does it mean a person will not say no. For some tolerance is associated with wishy-washy people.

The Scriptures speak directly to this tolerance issue: while I was yet a sinner God accepted me; unless your righteousness exceeds that of the scribes and pharisees; there is no difference between Jew or Greek, male or female, slave or free; we are one body with different gifts; to name just a few. Jesus was perhaps the most tolerant person ever to live. There was no ambiguity about what He believed or what He was about. In fact, a good case could be made about the intolerance of Jesus. He was intolerant of the way the money changers were using His Father's house. He was intolerant of the way people treated the poor and the outcast. Some of Jesus' most critical remarks were directed to those who were comfortable in their own religious world, whose spiritual life had become self-serving rather than God-serving. He was intolerant of the greed, injustice, pride, or any of the actions or attitudes that were contrary to peoples' relationship and devotion to God. His intolerance certainly created some negative reactions from those whose position He threatened.

But the difference between Jesus' intolerance and the intolerance people generally display is that his intolerance was always redemptive and cleansing in nature. Anything that would take people away from love of God and love of neighbor, Jesus would not tolerate. To those who were lost, hurting, or searching in life, Jesus could and would share compassion, understanding and healing. But to those who thought they knew the way, who were trying to show off their own religious grandiosity, or who were trying to protect their self-designed divine image, Jesus challenged and confronted. Jesus' intolerance was a prophetic call back to the divine mandate of doing what is just, of showing constant love, and of walking humbly with the Lord.

The tolerance that Jesus embodied was people centered. He was tolerant of the people that the world had discarded and written off. The tolerance that Jesus displayed came out of a genuine humility that marked all of Jesus' life. Jesus was the only person in the history of humankind that could truly love the sinner and hate the sin, without ending up hating both. Jesus was equally comfortable with the sinners and the outcast, the pharisees and the tax collectors. He accepted people right where they were. He allowed people to be who they were in His presence — people.

If Jesus allowed people to be different from Him, to say no to His invitation to discipleship, to follow their own course, and to choose or not choose Him, then people are probably moving away from His spirit when they practice intolerance. Intolerance is another way of playing God. Intolerance is a throw back to the narcissistic godness that people sometimes believe about themselves.

Alcoholics are familiar with this concept far better than others in the general public. When they were drinking, or using, their intolerance level was high. Since the whole world and his/her family revolves around the alcoholic the alcoholic demands, through words and actions, that all the world conform to him. The alcoholic becomes increasingly intolerant of the behavior and the feelings of others. Therefore, there is often a blow up over the smallest of things. Meals too early or too late, the toilet paper rolled the wrong way, things not in exact order. Everything and anything can set off the alcoholic.

Tim was a severe alcoholic. His wife Jenny was just beginning to come to terms with her codependency and her need to be in AlAnon. Tim was always focused on her and what she needed to be doing and how much she should be working on her program. Everything she did was wrong. He was upset because she wasn't meeting his needs. He thought that if only he could get her into line, their marriage and their problems would be over. He was laying all this out to another guy in the program, about how Jenny was always doing this or that. Finally the guy asked him how long it had taken him to get to this point. Tim said about three years. And then he went on to ask, "When are you going to let her have the space and time for her recovery that she has given you for yours?"

Intolerance walls people away from each other. Deep down it is not so much a matter of superiority that makes people intolerant as it is the deep seated inferiority that they feel about themselves. That was the way it was for Tim, and that is the way it is for others as well. Intolerance comes out of one's sense of isolation and loneliness. It is confining and restrictive. That is why the discovery of tolerance is so liberating. Tolerance is the release from all of the tension, conflict, manipulation, and hostility that was in control. Harry Tiebout explained it this way:

> The problems of inferiority and superiority drop out and in their stead patients think and feel in terms of 'live and let live', a state of mind which permits them to accept humbly and without rancor their difference from their fellows and at the same time permits them to accept the difference of their fellows from them. More over, along with this new capacity to 'live and let live', patients have a new ability to feel that way about themselves. They no longer drive themselves so vigorously nor criticize themselves so harshly which results in the disappearance of the perfectionistic tendency with its idealistic overtones. They not only become gentler with the world but gentler with themselves.[1]

It was early in the program history that the founders of AA struggled with their own tolerance, first to the alcohol and then to others around them. When they were drinking, the body's tolerance to alcohol was high. They would always drink more and longer than anyone else. More often than not, we have heard people say: "Boy he can drink 'till the cows come home. He can drink you right under the table. There's a guy who can really pound them home." Then as the disease progresses, the tolerance level drops, both on a physical level, and on an emotional, interpersonal, and spiritual level. There is a spiritual correlation to alcohol consumption and its effects, with tolerance and its effects. The greater a person's tolerance is for alcohol, the greater that person's intolerance will be toward self and others.

That's why tolerance is such an important step in the alcoholic's recovery and spiritual program. It opens the alcoholic up to himself and his perfectionism and demands on self and others. He begins to see that he is not what he thought he was all along. He does not have to be as tough on himself and others. He can be more open to others, their needs and the freedom and space they need. He can be more himself. The spiritual program of the alcoholic is one of self-acceptance and self-forgiveness. Once that is attained it can be extended to others. Tolerance means being comfortable enough with the self that one can be comfortable with others.

Tolerance in our spiritual life means that people begin to see that others are far more like them than different from them. They experience the variety of ways of doing, believing and thinking as a good thing.

At our church we have a Saturday morning AA group. It has grown to 75-80 people over the past five years. After their opening they break into three groups. There is a smoker's group, a group that goes in the nursery, and another group which meets in the sanctuary. In the sanctuary, seated near the altar, in the same space that on Sunday the congregation praises God, is a small group of AAer's. Within this group are Christians, agnostics, atheists — all people with a wide diversity of religious backgrounds. They are united not in their religion but in their common background, and their commitment to their spiritual growth and progress. At any given time that growth and progress can be different for different people, and that's okay. What works for one doesn't necessarily mean that it will work for another.

There is a common acceptance of one another. When and how they can help each other, they do. When they need to back off, they will. But what they have left behind at the entrance to the sanctuary, maybe even before they entered the church, is the need to change and convert one another. They have turned that job over to a higher power. They don't worry about all the differences that separate them. They see these variances and differences as opportunities to grow themselves. The differences no longer need to separate, but now, as they practice tolerance, the differences really unite and hold close.

As a religious agency, as a church, how many times do we see that kind of diversity and tolerance displayed within the church walls? Probably no where as often as in the AA group that meets on Saturday morning. Tolerance doesn't come easily like the other steps — it's not once and for all. It is a constant daily process. It does get somewhat easier on one hand, but on the other, it is always tough. There is always a desire to want to make others as close to a clone of oneself as possible. As one practices tolerance in all aspects they can see better both when they are intolerant and when they aren't.

Tolerance makes one freer with forgiveness, more open to others and their needs, more accepting for them for who they are, and better able to allow them the space they need. It gives one a greater capacity for love of self and others, and better enables one to watch and appreciate the rich variety in life the whole way through.

Chapter 13

Step Eleven:
Sharing The Story

"Tell me a story, Daddy, tell me about when you were a little boy like me. Tell me about when you and Uncle Rick were growing up on the farm. Tell me how you two used to go down to the creek to play and about the time you dammed up the creek so that Grandpa couldn't get across to the other side. And remember how mad Grandpa was when he found that. And he said that he didn't care how long it took you to build it, he was going to give you five minutes to tear it apart."

"Well, I already told you the story, Son." "That's OK, Dad, tell me again. I like it when you tell me stories."

When the old Rabbi was told by one of the members of the congregation how bad it was, he said, "It could always be worse." The man said, "It couldn't get worse than now." So the rabbi told him a story.

Two alcoholics were trying desperately to get sober. They had been preached at, they knew they needed help, but they could not stop. They heard and felt judgment from friends and family. But that did not stop their drinking, though it slowed it down from time to time. Most of it just reinforced the negative self image that they felt because of their increased drinking.

Then a third man joined them and began to share his story. He did not tell them how bad they were, what they were doing wrong. He only told them about where he had been, what had happened along that journey, how he felt about certain things, and what kind of things he was now doing to stay sober. As he told his story a rapport was established, a trust was extended, and finally they felt that someone was there who understood them. The important thing was, he never mentioned the two of them. He only talked about himself. It was out of the kinship and the friendship of one person talking to another that made the difference. But it was the relationship and the friendship that was established first.

A lot of important ingredients fell together in the formative state of AA. The understanding of the compulsion of the mind and the allergy of the body was instrumental in the spirituality that developed. The Jungian insight said that this was a hopeless disease unless one began to approach it from a spiritual center and that no one had any power over the disease. But as important as that was came also the discovery that the disease couldn't be cured alone. It took a Higher Power and the willingness to turn everything over to that Higher Power. But there was something more. Somehow, someway, there had to be a personal sharing of the story. It had to be real stories, daily stories, no-nonsense, sometimes, painful stories, but stories that had to be told. That is how one of the most important chapters of the Big Book got written. It was a sharing of personal stories of how it worked.

> This chapter, reflecting all that Bill and Dr. Bob had learned, offered not analysis but witness — the witness of their experience. The structure and style of this whole chapter in no way examined origin or causation — of alcoholism or of its cure. The simple format was 'This is what we did,' a sharing of experience, drinking and sober.[1]

There is something about stories that make them worth listening to. People may know the story, they may have heard it a hundred times before. But they want to hear it again. In stories there is an identity and an identification with others.

When Jesus was doing His ministry, the power of His imagery was created in the stories He told. It allowed the listener to make up his mind for himself what the meaning was and how to apply it to his own life. If the listener took the story and applied it, that would be great. But at the same time there was no way to dispute what was said. If the listener dismissed the story, the teller was no less for telling it. That is not the case with all teaching. When a teacher tries to get across a point and impart information and the student does well, the teacher must have done a good job. However, if the student does poorly then the teacher must be bad. Not so with stories.

Stories stand on their own. They come out of experiences of life and people's reflections on them and the meaning they give them. There is no right or wrong experience, only the experience as it stands.

> *At the very heart of all the experience of Alcoholics Anonymous lay experience. To be shared, something first had to be possessed. 'You can keep it only by giving it away,' but 'You have to have it before you can give it.' What was being talked about was 'new life' — the heart of the 'born again' or 'twice-born,' understanding inherent in all Evangelical religion.*[2]

Stories are as much for the benefit of the teller as for those who listen. In our family at every family gathering there is story time. No, it is not at bedtime. The stories are usually told around the dinner table. They are stories of growing up and stories about the things we tried to pull over on our parents, stories about living on the farm. They are stories of past family events. These stories are looked forward to. Mostly they are family history that we all know by heart. In fact, we all take turns telling them. One story leads into another. The stories have come to identify us. These stories tell who we are and what we value. They share those important events in our family history — even if the important event was as mundane as stopping at three Dairy Queens on a trip to town and back.

As people share their stories, there is a common ground where their lives meet. There are certainly parts of one person's story that have no value or interest to another. But in those parts of a person's story that touched another's story, there is an interest and a bonding that takes place. It is the beginning of a relationship that can transcend differences in culture, status, vocation, stations in life and whatever previous differences there were.

About ten years ago, at an Illinois Synod Convention of the LCA, the Social Ministry Committee report consisted of a man coming to the podium to share his story. Usually committee reports are boring and filled with facts about how many things were done during the course of the year. Most of the time, they are repetitious and of little consequence. This time, a man in a flannel shirt with long sideburns got up to speak. This guy was different. He began by saying "My name is Bob and I am an alcoholic." He began to describe his struggle for sobriety. At first people paid Bob no more or less attention than anyone else. But as the story went on more people became interested in his personal struggle. He shared his family problems and how his wife had left him. As the story went on, people's conversations dropped. As he continued his story, people in the convention hall had tears in their eyes. The convention hall was completely silent. There was no movement. Bob's story was the focus. Even the toughest skeptics were biting their lips as Bob described how God in Jesus Christ had saved his life and his marriage. Stories have power in and of themselves and stories change people.

That's what happened when Randy and I were counselling together. We had worked together on his problems for nearly two years. Some progress was made. We gained insight into his family and his own personal history. He and his wife were on the verge of separation again. They had been at that point before. But one Wednesday afternoon Randy came into the church and just sat. He waited for me to be free and come into the office. He said that he and his wife were fighting. He felt that no matter what he did it was wrong. We had talked from time to time about his drinking and his wife's involvement in AlAnon. He asked me if I thought his drinking was a problem. "What are you asking?" I said. "Do I think you are an alcoholic? I can't say. This is not my judgment to make. All I can say is there is alcoholism in your family. Your mom probably died because of alcohol related physical problems. There seems to be a problem between you and your wife and it always seems to be alcohol related." But now what? We were at an impasse. We had been there before. It seemed we could never get beyond this impasse. So I called a friend in AA. I asked Russ if he would meet me and Randy at my office. The next day, the three of us sat there with our coffee looking at one another. After a few moments of silence, Russ said "The Padre asked me to come today to talk with you. It sounds like there may be some problems in your home, many of which are alcohol related. Before we get going I have to tell you about what has happened to me." He went on to describe his drinking, about how everyone at the bar would agree on what a bitch he had for a wife, about how alcohol was a prevalent problem in his family of origin, about the love/hate relationship he had developed with his wife, and about what it had done to his children. As Randy listened you could see denial and resistance in his eyes, but there was also identification and acceptance. When Russ finished telling the story he was ready to listen to Randy's. However, he made Randy look at his denial and expose his resistance. The next day Randy began AA. Randy has said since then, "I know where those people are coming from, their stories link with mine."

From the beginning of the Christian faith, stories have been the center, not only to the ministry and teaching of Jesus, but to the life of His followers as well. These stories are a personal witness of how and when the presence of God has made a difference. Some Christian denominations have gotten away from stories for too long. Their emphasis has been on right doctrine and systematic theology. Being able to work through a systematic theology is vital and a part of gaining a greater understanding of the Christian faith. Academic knowledge has been one of the great strengths of my Lutheran seminary education. Many people have been drawn toward the Lutheran Church because of its high academic standards. But sometimes we have forgotten that knowledge can come through other means. Knowledge comes from both one's head and one's heart. The power of faith can be just as effective or even more effective when it is shared in a story. After all, most people, at least in the church know the doctrine, they know the difference between right and wrong, they are familiar with the biblical witness. Stories put flesh and blood on the doctrinal truths, which help as other believers seek to live out these truths and apply them to their lives.

There is a story of a young man who was enamored by all that he was learning in seminary. He had been particularly impressed by the writing of Paul Tillich. One of Tillich's central contributions was the idea of ultimate concern. Well, this young man was bursting at the seams wanting to tell others about this wonderful insight he had gained.

So at home over the Christmas break, he went to visit an old friend of his who was filled with wisdom and understanding, even though he had never gone beyond the sixth grade. As the young man began to explain this ultimate concern, his old friend listened with interest. The young man described the fact that the ultimate concern was whatever you lifted up to be the most important thing in life. He told his old friend that whatever is the most important thing in your life is your god. Money could be your ultimate concern, or status, or power. So can the acquiring and accumulation of things. These things will then be your god because they are your ultimate concern. "Are you following this so far?" he asked. The old man looked at him and said "Yes, I'm following." The young man was so pleased that he could impress the man whom many had looked up to through the years. "By the way," the young man went on. "What is your ultimate concern?" The old man looked off a moment or two, and then back at his young friend. And he simply said "My ultimate concern is that the ultimate is concerned about me."

That is where it is for most people. It is almost impossible to share that through doctrine alone. That comes only through stories that are shared when believers, spiritual travellers, can tell and give witness to where they have experienced the ultimate concern for them. Maybe that is why testimonies have been such an important part of the Baptist church's tradition. The testimony is no more than a personal story where and when the believer experiences God in his or her life.

Maybe that is the real difference. Doctrine is focused on the "what" of God. And that "what" is always subject to different interpretation, emphasis, and understanding. The "what" of God leads to the "if" of God. Trying to define God leaves people with the interminable question if God exists, if God is there, if God really makes a difference in life and living. When people center attention on the "what" — what does God look like, what is God doing, where is God, what is God really up to — then those answers can be subject to all kinds of questions and all kinds of disputes. The "what" questions keeps God out there away from one's personal experience and personal world. God will always remain remote, distant, and truly undefined as long as one depends on the accumulation of enough information, whether one can study hard enough, have enough precision, so one can have the one true answer. If that is a person's attitude, his or her God will have to be pretty close to all others because every person feels they have a lock on the truth.

Stories refocus one's thoughts and attention to the "when" of God. Matthew 25 asks "when." "When have we seen you hungry, naked, thirsty or in prison?" And Jesus replies, "When you have done this to the least of these my brothers you have done it to me." Story takes seriously the "when" of God. "It is just like when . . ." God is no longer an object to be studied, categorized, compartmentalized, or an objective point of interest. The story moves God from out there to in here. As Martin Buber would say, it moves the God/human dimension from an I/it relationship to an I/thou relationship. In order to tell the story of God a person needs to share the when. And in sharing the when of God one also is telling the story of God.

This includes those times when God is active and alive, as well as those times when God seems dormant or dead. It includes times when God is speaking, as well as when God is silent. It takes into account when God is caring and close, as well as when God is remote and indifferent. The story can speak to all of the "whens" of God, and probably includes some or all of them. There is a time when God moved very dramatically in life. There is a time that God was absent. Either way the story stands and people can identify and relate.

Several months ago we had a women's service at church. I asked one of the women to preach the sermon. I had asked her a year before if she would be willing to preach. She said she needed a whole year to prepare. Two weeks before the service, she came in to my office in a panic. She had read the commentaries, but she could not think of anything more to say. And then I told her the reason I had asked her was because I thought she had a powerful personal story about the importance of God in her life. That is what she prepared and shared, and it was powerful. The day after services, I asked another woman to preach next year. She went into an incredible panic. "No, no, I could never do that. I don't have anything to say. There is no way that I can do anything like that." But she went home that afternoon and began to write. By the next morning she had it. It was her story. She said she is not sure she can share it in front of others. In fact, she had an idea that we should include one of these stories in each month's newsletter. In fact, what she wrote is so magnificent that I wish I could include it in this paper.

It has been interesting to see how people like Frederick Beuchner, Garrison Keilor, Walter Wangerin, Robert Fulhgum and others have brought such credibility to the story and story preaching. There has been a renewed interest and emphasis on story preaching. People are sitting at the feet of these master story tellers, listening for the insight, the touch and the wonder of the story. They have helped re-establish the story as a legitimate art form that can touch the hearts and lives of millions of people.

When you get into personal spiritual lives, the real key is to begin to separate The Story from a story. In a story, anything will do. A story might entertain or edify or even assume or challenge. A story could be any story. But within one's own personal spiritual life there is a listening for "THE" story. "The" story has to do with salvation. As the old hymn puts it, "I love to tell the story, the old, old story." We don't have to find the new. The old, old story is told because familiarity is something that brings security. We tell the story to dwell in it. It is like certain books that my four-year-old has. He knows the words, he knows the story better than the reader. Yet he loves the story precisely because there is comfort.

For spiritual life to grow and to develop, a person constantly looks for ways one's personal story intersects with The Story. It is this story of salvation that shapes and gives form and meaning to a person's story. At least, biblically speaking, the story is the Holy History, the action of God in people's lives. As one begins to understand where the personal story that belongs to "me and me alone" and The Story touch, then one can share a new story in a very personal way. That is what AA folks intuitively understand. They have been to the bottom. They are aware of the life and death matters before them. They discovered almost by accident that it is by sharing the story that there is hope and healing.

As people share the story with one another, there is benefit for both the tellers and the listeners, for the givers and the receivers. In fact, if the truth be known, the greater benefit is for the one who is doing the sharing. This sharing of the story is an important step because the teller really needs to tell this for her or himself. To a slightly lesser degree the teller

149

needs to tell this for someone else. It is in telling the story that a relationship is possible. Here is where life has been lived, the road that has been trod, and the strengths and weaknesses of that journey. The real tragedy is that there are very few who can share of themselves that deeply. There is no one who can bear their chemical dependency alone, just as there is no one who can be a Christian alone. One cannot be a Christian isolated from the community of faith, and the ongoing story of that community.

It is in the telling of one's own very unique and personal story that others can see and appreciate the uniqueness as well as the common ground and common humanity that hold all people together. Each of the stories that are told will give listeners an awareness of all that has gone on around and within the teller.

As the story is shared, hearts and lives are touched and it creates a new awareness and positive identification with the teller. When that happens there is the possibility of change. And it is in change that we grow in our spirituality.

Chapter 14

Step Twelve:
Movement Beyond Self

Diane grew up in an alcoholic family. She and her Pastor had been counseling for four months. During that time she worked on trying to understand herself and her family. She was a very shy and self-conscious person. This was the first church she had been a part of. During that time she had struggled with her family of origin. It was always her role to take care of her family. Even though she was thirty years old she had always lived at home. Both she and her brother were financially, as well as emotionally, responsible for their depressed and dependent mother. In the past several years, their mother had become progressively worse.

However, Diane had come to an awareness of how codependent she really was. She and her Pastor worked long and hard at helping her make the decision to move out so that she could begin a life on her own. Often she complained that she had no life. Slowly, ever so slowly, she began to take steps that would help her realize her goal.

After some small talk the Pastor asked, "So what do you want to talk about today?" There was a long silence. Finally Diane asked, "Do you think I'm self-centered?" "I don't know, what do you think?" Diane was obviously uncomfortable with the return question. She went on to say, "God, it is tough. I know what others feel better than I know what I feel. It is easy for me to grab on to what others want me to be. I feel like I can get into others so much better than I can myself. Yet I feel that when we talk in here we only talk about me, me, . . . me! It seems like I am so wrapped up in myself and my problems. You know, my world is so small it is really frightening." Then the Pastor said, "Do you really want me to answer that question?" She nodded. "Well, then the answer is yes and no." "Yes, you are self-centered, but no, you're not. Both are true." She smiled in relief and said, "That's what I think, too." From that point on Diane began a quest to move beyond herself. But Diane's question is really other people's question as well. As Carl Whitaker says:

> *My conviction is that we are all as dishonest as the standard politician; we are all talking out of both sides of our mouths, making believe that we are not the center of our own worlds. We carefully conceal our personal lives and maintain an artificially constructed social facade that is essentially dishonest.*[1]

The core concept of AA focuses on the selfishness and the self-centeredness that is so much a part of human nature. There is a natural tendency for people, even the most benevolent, to be self directed and self-serving. It is so easy to turn things in on the self. There is a Diane in us all. Perhaps those who are alcoholic or those who come from alcoholic families are only different from anyone else to the degree that the self centeredness is apparent and life disrupting. Others have a better way of covering up the me-centeredness and are not as honest in dealings with self and others. Carl Whitaker is always reminding his readers and his students, as well as his clients, that he is in the therapy business basically for himself. For if he is not helping himself and growing in the counseling sessions, there is probably little that he can really do for others.

The last step in the spiritual journey is the step that goes beyond the self. It is the last step because so much must happen before one can really reach out to others in a healthy self-differentiated way. Until one has worked through all the other steps first, there is no way a person can ever get beyond the self. Even when people are great caretakers, or will sacrifice their own well being and goals for years, it does not mean that they get beyond themselves.

That is the funny thing about this. Without a solid spiritual center, all efforts to reach out remain self-directed and self-defeating. There is really no outward direction in people's lives without a strong spiritual center and direction.

Tony was leading an AA meeting. It was an open topic meeting. So he began talking about the pain he had in his life, the emotional pain he experienced trying to live a sober life, and trying to live in a marriage that caused a lot of strain. He spoke of the physical pain of rehab from the injuries incurred in a recent accident. About half way through his sharing, a young woman hobbled into the meeting, using a cane that supported her fragile weight. She sat down near the back. When Tony finished, several others took their turns speaking about different and unrelated topics, some dealing with pain, some not. It came to that young woman. Not only was she crippled by a limp, she had a difficult time speaking because part of her face was paralyzed. She introduced herself, apologized for being late, and then asked if pain was the topic. She went on to say she knew a lot about pain. She, too, had been in a severe car accident which almost killed her. She spent a long time in the intensive care unit at the hospital. While she was there, she suffered a stroke that almost killed her. As she told her story, tears streamed down her face. Her story was passionate, her questions about where God was were deeply probing, her expression of pain was genuine. She made it clear she was reaching out for help. When she finished, she thanked everyone for listening. The next person to speak talked of something totally different and unrelated. The following person did the same. Two more people spoke about the fears of the holidays and what they were going to do in order to handle their drunken relatives. Finally, the fifth man to speak, began by saying, "You know you have heard two people share their pain, and their request for help, and no one has even acknowledged their pain or their hurt. You people are talking shit. I'm sorry if this sounds judgmental but you're just talking shit and that's all there is to it. If we of all people can't get out of our little self-centered worlds, God help us all." Maybe that sounds vulgar. But, how perceptive! How wonderfully articulate. How magnificently honest. Selfishness and self-centeredness are at the root of the spiritual malady of people. Even though s/he will often disagree, it is the self gone wild that is cause of so much pain for the alcoholic. It is only through the help of God and the surrender of any attempts at playing God that will ever allow people to move out into the world with any degree of health and wholeness.

That story could also be repeated in many Christian congregations. Indifference, apathy, and self-centeredness, are just as difficult for Christians to struggle with, as anyone else. Getting beyond oneself takes a great deal of spiritual groundwork before it happens. Sometimes, Christians have so little compassion for the plight of others that it is astounding. Sometimes Christians have so little identification with the pain of others that it is almost a sin. Sometimes they fail to listen to the pain of the world around them. So much of congregational time and energy gets absorbed in trivial pet projects that the pain of those who are hurting goes unnoticed. It is not just individuals who cannot get beyond themselves. Entire churches can be the same way. It is no wonder that the world often criticizes the church for only "talking shit" and not being able to get beyond itself.

Religious people, good people, decent people so often cannot get beyond themselves. They look to see if their needs are being fulfilled. It is as if the church represents a surrogate parent and, as long as it is fulfilling the needs of the individual, it must be fulfilling the religious need.

As a pastor, I hear it all the time. A young woman came into my office a month or so ago. I had not seen her in about

154

What AA has discovered is that in a very real way the sobriety of the alcoholic is dependent upon taking that message to the world. They do not just adopt a sober lifestyle and continue to focus on it to improve the self alone. They found that people had to get back out into life. In AA the spread of the movement was not intended to be for a specialized group of ordained missionaries. It was not something to which you could say, "No thanks, it's not my gift." It was not something that one did only after enough formal training and knowledge was received. It is part of each individual's program almost from the beginning. It is something one does for self as much as for others. AA is often called a selfish program. But as a woman in the program told me, "We must better ourselves in order to be better to and for others." People will not always be successful and change others. That doesn't always happen. But the message has to get out and it gets out best through people in the program, one on one.

The same is true of the Christian church as well. It is the nature of the church to go beyond itself. Just as the alcoholic goes beyond self to maintain sobriety, so too, does the church go beyond itself to maintain and grow in its spirituality.

> *The need to escape the private prison of the narrow self is one of the themes that undergirds and finds expression in all the great religions of mankind. That human life has meaning, ultimate meaning, only as lived for others — or for an Other — seems one way of understanding the deep unity as well as the profound variety of the human experience termed 'religious.' Fundamental to all human existence seems the quest for self-transcendence.* [3]

That is the paradox of spirituality and religion at its best. To find life one must lose life. One becomes great by serving. People are blessed to the degree that they are a blessing to others.

The church and the religious community has to relearn and reemphasize this step. It is far too easy to let the other person do it, to pay the hired staff to do it, to wait for someone else

157

to move first to reach out. The prayer of St. Francis begins, "Lord, make me an instrument of Your peace!" Christians are not only instruments of God's peace, they are channels of God's love, they are reflections of God's light and representatives of God's presence. God acts in and through people, not only in the dramatic and earthshaking events of this world. Few have much opportunity or much talent for those kind of things. But people do have tremendous opportunities to display and share God's love and presence with those with whom they share life on a day to day basis. To the question, "Where do we find God?" Harold Kushner offers this:

> *'Wherever justice is meted out to the powerless, wherever people share their bread with the hungry, extend freedom to the oppressed, lend a hand to the afflicted, the lonely, and the stranger, God is present.' Why else would people be generous, brave, honest, or helpful? Why would people give away their money, contribute their energy and free time, take on the establishment power structure unless God were at work through them?*[4]

Too often people worry about doing great things, and forget that their call is to do things in great love. Whenever and wherever people embody these qualities, God is present. Kushner goes on to say that instead of asking the question of, "Where is God?" a better question would be "When is God?" "Being in God's presence is not a matter of being in the right place but of doing the right things."[5] It is the presence of God that moves people beyond themselves in a way that seeks to care and share for those in need in whatever way. This statement from John Powell is powerful: "Now I believe much more simply that when we love, God's grace flows into this world through the channel of our love: healing it, straightening its twistedness, mending its brokenness, and enlightening its darkness. We are only God's instruments."[6] In the hands of an artisan, a craftsman, a surgeon, an instrument brings beauty and joy to life. Each person can be an instrument of God's peace, and of God's love.

Within the Christian community, there is a renewed emphasis on seeing Christ in the world. There is a renewed awareness that as Christians reach out to those beyond them, they are really reaching out to Christ Himself. The Christ is in all of us. People often spend time looking for Christ in gothic cathedrals, in the wondrous beauty of nature, in the amazing complexities of the universe. But Christ is most often found in the least, the lost, the outcast, and the suffering, the lonely and the hungry. There is where Christ is to be found. That is the movement He calls people to. As they move beyond themselves to friends and family, to strangers and the homeless, they are really moving closer to God in Christ.

Being religious does not mean Christians have memorized all the prayers and can recite the formalized rituals and adhere to all the correct doctrines. Being religious means that Christians put on a new set of glasses. They see the world and others differently, from the eyes and perspective of Christ himself. There is Christ in each and every person they come in contact with each day.

Christmas is the movement of God to humankind. This movement is called the Incarnation. God became visible in a tangible human form. The twelfth step is the incarnation of Christ from one person to another. The message takes on flesh. By his very presence something happens on a personal and interpersonal plane. For the alcoholic the message bringer becomes a symbol of hope. To those who are outside the fellowship of the church, the message bringer is the incarnation of the very love of God. The movement to others is nothing less than the movement of Christ in this world.

This step is a movement beyond the self. The world is really a very frightening place. People might not like who the Christian is. They may slam the door in the Christian's face. They might not respond in the way hoped or wanted. They may choose a path that leads to further destruction and to greater pain and isolation. That is their choice. It is not up to the individual to convert or impose his standards or values on others, just as it is not up to that person to make anyone sober. Both are works of God. As a pastor, I am not in charge of church growth, just as I am not in charge of another's sobriety. I am not God. I cannot tell a person that s/he must come to church, neither can I tell them they have to follow the AA way. All that can be offered is a sharing what both have done and meant. This step says there is nobody who can play God. The best anyone can do is to give witness to the difference spirituality makes in life. Hopefully personal spirituality is a matter of attraction and not just promotion. Every person has the job to go and tell and reach out in the love of Christ, and to share what they have seen and heard, and invite others to share in the joy and fellowship that they have experienced. The rest is up to God and the person's job is to entrust it to God's care and keeping.

Chapter 15

Conclusion

I know my spirituality has been increased and strengthened through the friendships, the sharing, and the caring of AA members to and for me. I have been blessed, changed, and moved because of my relationship with them. In turn I hope that they have felt the same from me. It is through both the Church and AA that God is seeking to make His presence known, to bring healing and wholeness, and to embody a message of hope and peace, of love and salvation. As long as I take one day and one step at a time, it will work.

In AA the word "work" has taken on special significance and meaning. Many times I have heard a person in AA tell another simply, "it works." What makes this true and concrete is the fact that the Twelve Steps is the only therapy that dares to write its program in the past tense. That means they are proven steps because they have already worked for those who have adhered to them. When asked about past failures and slips, the same person might say, "It was because I didn't work my program the first time."

Among the many things that AA has taught me is that spirituality takes work. It is not something that one is born with, or that some people have more of than others. Spirituality is learned. Without the effort, time, discipline, and the work spirituality forever remains in an embryonic state. That work does pay off. Lives do change. Miracles do happen. God does take charge. Working the program has helped people look at themselves, others, and their Higher Power differently.

But does this spirituality apply just to those in AA, or is there a broader appeal? Can those who are not alcoholic use these tools and benefit from the spiritual framework from which to build their own spiritual home?

The goal and purpose of spirituality is to increase one's joy, peace, contentment, and self worth. AA talks about these things all the time. Meetings revolve around the topics of what happens when these emotions are absent, and the steps that need to be taken to restore and renew these special states of being. What these are really talking about is the gifts of the Spirit. When these gifts are present, the fruits of the Spirit are the result.

This paper has used the alcoholic as a paradigm of spiritual growth and life. That paradigm has been instrumental in the physical recovery and the spiritual awakening of hundreds of thousands of alcoholics. This author would contend that the paradigm has a far broader appeal than to just the alcoholic. The opening chapter of this paper began with a man lost in the woods. It is out of that lostness that people in AA have made important discoveries. If this research had been done in a lab, it would have been hailed for its exactness, even though it did not necessarily use empirical statistical methods. For within AA as within all human nature there are far too many variables. There are variables of the personality, of the pull to drink, of the power of the ego, of other family members, of negative human emotions controlling one's behavior. The painful discoveries that people in AA have made are the experiences they have had in living without their Higher Power. They have made some important discoveries about the human spirit as well as the divine spirit. As a result they are brutally honest about both.

In order to describe what is happening, imagine two concentric circles, an outer circle that would represent behavior, and an inner circle that would include feelings. The behavior circle would include all of the defensive reactions that a person uses to protect himself from the painful feelings or the possibility of painful feelings in the inner circle. Within the behavior circle are unique ways of reacting, as well as ways of reacting that are common to everyone. As a counselor, I pay attention to the behavior. It is a clue to what is going on. When certain behaviors are put together, they form a pattern. Behavior points to that which is going on within a person, or between people.

Using the alcoholic again, certain patterns in an individual give a clue that the alcohol may be a problem. Just as those same patterns mean something else for other family members. When other affected members act in certain ways, there is a fairly good signal that they are codependent and equally stuck in the disease. But behavior is indicative when other problems are present as well. There are behavioral symptoms when a person is stuck in grief, or when stress has overwhelmed a person, or when depression is in control, or when locked by painful childhood memories. Though each individual will have unique ways of behaving, ways of coping, ways of handling their life, there still are enough similarities with others that allow researchers to characterize actions as alcoholic behavior, or grief reaction, or stress symptoms and the like.

In that inner circle are the feelings. How these feelings are acted out will be different from person to person. But whether one is dealing with alcoholism, grief, stress, depression, many of the feelings and the emotions that trigger them is the same. Whereas one person may take a childhood pain and become an alcoholic, another may become chronically depressed, another may build up intense resentment for the opposite sex, another may forever have difficulty in attaining any positive lasting relationships, and still another may forever mourn that lost childhood. Each of them is responding to the same inner feelings that are experienced by all, which include hurt, shame, loneliness, guilt, fear, inadequacy, confusion. These are the

163

feelings that are shared at an AA meeting, they are the feelings that are worked through in therapy, they are the feelings dealt with in the Christian scriptures and faith.

Since the inner feelings are common to all people, the spiritual steps should work with all as well. Though the symptomology may be different, with some more acute, some more chronic, a spiritual approach that touched the shared feeling level should be workable for not only alcoholics but non-alcoholics as well.

The twelve steps outlined in this paper will work for all, because they relate to the personal feeling world that is part and parcel of everyone.

Let me walk with you, the reader, how this will work in a non-alcoholic person and situation.

Gary and Gail were expecting their second baby. Both were near thirty years old, and were quite excited. Gail followed the strict nutritional diet and exercise guidelines that she had received from her doctor. The birth of her first child five years before had gone smoothly, producing a healthy son. But on one of her last check ups late in this pregnancy, the doctor reported that she could find no heartbeat. The medical team decided that they would induce labor the next day. That was the longest twenty-four hours that Gary and Gail had ever spent. The next morning, the doctors again checked for a heartbeat. There was none. Gary was able to read through the tears a pamphlet entitled ''When Hello Means Goodbye'' which helped them prepare for the stillbirth of their baby. Late that afternoon, Gail gave birth to a beautiful baby girl, registered in the medical records as stillborn.

Step one in the spiritual journey is crisis. It is the awareness that things are not working the way they are suppose to work. Somehow things that had gone smoothly before are now unworkable. Old answers that used to be satisfactory are now more like questions. Personal resources for coping are limited. There is nothing more one can do. It is a bottoming out. The world caves in. For Gary and Gail that happened on that fateful

Tuesday. The crisis was precipitated by the stillbirth of their daughter. What could they do? What would they do? They could continue down further into the bleak solitude of their own grief. They could forever question, blame, even rage at God, and others for taking their little daughter. They could forever remain suspended in that painful moment. When people are in a crisis, they often believe there are no positive or healthy choices or options available. "I'm this way because I have to." "Can't you see this is the way I have to be because of what happened?" "I won't let this affect me, I'm stronger, I can go it alone, I can take care of myself." But there is a different choice available. The choice is really a choice of if and how one's spiritual road will take them. Gary and Gail used this crisis to travel the spiritual road out of their grief.

Step One questions for reflection:

1. What are the three most difficult crises of your life?
2. What crises have repeated?
3. What have your crises done to or for you?
4. What defense mechanisms have you used to keep you out of crises?
5. How and what spiritual resources have brought you strength?

The second step of spirituality is surrender. As has been pointed out in Chapter Four, the alcoholic has to surrender before there is any movement in the spiritual recovery. "I don't have a problem, the world has the problem," is the alcoholic attitude. The opposite of surrender is denial. From those who have studied death reaction, denial is the single strongest force on holding people back from working through their grief. When the alcoholic is in denial he will play all kinds of mind, emotional and behavioral games in order to pretend there is no problem. The same is true in death. Denial is powerful in grief. People say there must have been a reason, God must have wanted that child, you're better off not to have known the child, don't look at the child or hold it, because it will be way too hard on you, maybe you had better go somewhere where you can forget this horrible thing that has happened.

But denial does not leave the mind or emotions alone. It works on them constantly even when a person is not aware.

For Gary and Gail, the temptation was to deny that the birth ever happened, that their daughter was important, that they could love this child. There in the hospital room, they surrendered. They surrendered as they held their daughter, as they took pictures, as they named her a very special family name they had picked out. Here they surrendered their child to the death that had taken her. There they surrendered to the reality of what had taken place and the overwhelming pain and sorrow they felt. There they surrendered to the powerful feelings of sadness and emptiness. There they surrendered the fact that life was for them forever changed, and hopes and dreams would never be realized. There they surrendered to the fact that they needed a Higher Power to carry them through. Though they surrendered there that day, they would have to replay this step many more times in the future. As they surrendered they became weak, admitted they were defeated, and that they could not control over the situation. Surrender is the acceptance of that which we neither want or understand, and that which we have no power over to make different. Surrender meant for Gary and Gail connecting with their higher power that they call God in Christ to see them through.

Step Two questions for reflection:

1. What situations have made you feel completely defeated?

2. What battle(s) inside of you is causing pain?

3. What would happen if you completely surrendered your battle over to your higher power?

4. What prevents you from surrendering?

5. How is your EGO easing God out?

When we think of conversion, the third step, there may be a certain bewilderment here. Certainly conversion is wanted and even deemed necessary for the alcoholic. There are those drinking days, and then the sober days. Their before and after stories in AA leave no doubt as to the need for conversion

166

for them. With Gary and Gail, there was no days prior. They had always been good Christians. Theirs was a crisis of inordinant proportions. The emotions and feelings, the sadness and emptiness could have easily destroyed them as individuals and together as a couple. Conversion is a changing of negative attitudes and emotions into positive ones. For Gary and Gail, as for most people conversion is a reflective process. As they looked back on the events in the delivery room, the prayers offered by the chaplain, the presence of family and friends, they saw God present. The process of conversion continued as a woman who had also lost a baby just happened to be one of the attending nurses. She came in many times to talk with Gail about her feelings and emotions surrounding the loss of a child. Slowly Gary and Gail began to come to an acceptance of what had occurred. Conversion is a transformation of all those negative emotions into ones that are positive and growth enhancing. The Christian theological affirmation is that God can use bad for good, and that God, in all things, works for good for those that love him.

Tiebout lists the preconversion states of an individual as unstable, tense, nervous, afraid, guilty, ashamed, uncertain and unworthy. That is the depth of all human suffering. Those feelings could well be the feelings shared in the loss of a child or a loved one. Conversion brings a feeling of peace, safety, contentment, thankfulness, cleansing, saneness, receptive, prayerfulness. Restoring those feelings are also the goal of grief work. When one has experienced those kinds of changes in attitudes and feelings, a conversion no less than that of the Apostle Paul's has taken place. For that kind of acceptance and progress to be made, a spiritual conversion has to take place. In the year since their daughter's stillbirth, Gary and Gail are progressing in their conversion experience. Most conversions do take time. For a conversion to take hold, there has to be others around to walk with the person, to listen, to interpret their own spiritual experience and how far if little they have come thus far.

For Gary and Gail nothing had changed, but they had. There was no way to bring back their daughter. Her death was a reality. God had been present throughout, helping them reach out, and reestablishing communication with friends and family. Though the world was not conformed to them, somehow, Gary and Gail are being transformed. That is conversion.

Step Three questions for reflection:

1. What are the negatives controlling you?

2. Which of the preconversion emotions on Tiebout's list do you experience on a regular basis?

3. Where has your life journey been interrupted?

4. Who are the people God is using to bring about a conversion in you?

5. What attitudes, behaviors, emotions still need a conversion experience in you?

With death, the emptiness is so much a part of the process. That is why it is such an important step in the spiritual journey. That emptiness is scary. It is frightening to lose that much control. Surely there must be something one can do. Since emptiness brings with it the pain of uncertainty, there must be a drug to take, or a drink or two that will calm the nerves and take the edge off. Our culture tells us that emptiness and the experiences of emptiness are to be avoided at all costs. Gary and Gail stayed with the emptiness. They held their daughter for three hours. They put on the dress that she was to wear for baptism, but now would be worn for the funeral service. They said it would have been easier not to look, not to hold, not to stay with their child, but now they are glad they did. They said their experience was strange, in that the stillbirth makes them empty, but it was out of the emptiness that room was made in their hearts for the love of their daughter.

Step Four questions for reflection:

1. What is the emptiness inside of me that needs to be explored?

2. What are three things I need to empty myself of now to move along the spiritual road?

3. In my praying, am I doing more talking or listening?

4. What false fronts and illusions of myself am I trying to project on to others?

5. What am I doing with the silent places of my life?

Whenever a car hits a chuck hole while driving down the road, it is very easy for the alignment to be messed up. Crisis, tragedy, drinking, problems, stress all are things that knock people out of line and therefore off center. That makes for a shaky drive and hard steering. That is equally true in one's spiritual life, and is why recentering is the fifth step. For Gary and Gail, that stillbirth set life off center. They questioned God, their faith, their trust in the hospital and the staff. Grief does knock people off center, and mourning is the process of recentering. When the focus of life is only on the pain and loss, nothing else matters. For weeks after, Gary and Gail had little energy to do anything. Everything was a tremendous effort. They had little desire to go outside of the safety of the house. Even grocery shopping became a chore. The following Sunday, there was a rose on the altar at church, which was a way that church announced the birth of a child in the congregation. When the announcement was made, it was more than Gail could take, so she ran out of church. In the weeks following neither Gary or Gail could enter the room they had so lovingly prepared for their daughter. They intuitively knew that life was off center. They began talking to others who had lost children. They read the Psalms, particularly the ones that cried out to God in pain, and expressed the feeling of the absence of God. They prayed prayers that articulated their pain and sorrow. Slowly their lives are being recentered. Their process of recentering has made them rethink their image of God and reevaluate what they believed of life and death and life eternal. The people in their church, through their supportive presence helped them appreciate their faith in a whole new way. Their quiet time helped them see that they needed time every day to get refocused. They have done a lot more reading and reflecting about the meaning of life and the importance of relationships. Their pain drove them deeper into their center which is God. Their spiritual centeredness helped them look for a hopeful future, a greater dependency on God to sustain them, and to an acceptance of what happened.

Step Five questions for reflection:

1. What events, emotions or pressures set you off center?

2. Right now is your life in balance or is too much weight shifted in one way?

3. How much true quiet time do you take each day?

4. Draw a circle. Now divide the circle in pie-shaped wedges according to how much time, energy, focus you give to body, mind, spirit, work, family, pleasure, self, others. Is that the way you want the pie divided? What changes are needed to bring more balance?

5. On a scale of one to ten, how close do you feel to God? What steps might you take to narrow the distance?

Pain makes a person contract, pull back, withdraw. That is true whether the pain is physical or emotional. There is an almost instinctual response mechanism to protect oneself from danger and pain. Vulnerability, which is step six, makes love possible. The more a person loves, the greater the risk is that s/he will be hurt. It takes a great deal of spiritual strength to be totally vulnerable with another. Gary and Gail learned through their experience that life was painful. The naivete of before was dashed by the cruel facts of reality. The open positive trust displayed in life and with each other now became filled with cynicism and suspicion. They saw that it was a myth that tragedy brings couples together. Each was in pain, their own pain. They were expecting the other to reach out for help and support. But when none came, they got angry with each other and with themselves. There was a distance between them not there before. At the same time they withdrew from God. "Who could trust a God who let this happen?" The house became a symbol of what was going on inside of them. Shades were pulled down, doors remained closed, telephones were disconnected, visitors were put off and very little was spoken between the two of them. Then they received a card from a friend. It said, "Pain is the experience that makes room for more love in your heart." Gary and Gail began to realize that risking love opens one up to the possibility of being wounded, of being injured by another, and the willingness to put one's very life in the hands of another. Slowly at first, the window shades went up, the telephone reconnected, contact with the outside world and with each other was reestablished. Through visits from their Pastor, they began to renew lines of openness and communication with one another. They relearned sensitivity and empathy for each other and what it would take to maintain it. Their vulnerability helped them see their need for each other and that they couldn't go it alone. They began to talk of their pain, share their perspective on this very personal loss. They have come to appreciate how each hurts the same, but differently. As they have become more vulnerable with each other, they are exposing deep parts of their personality, their fears, insecurities, and feelings to each other and to God. But they say that family and friends still don't know how to handle the situation. In fact Gail's mother has not accepted the death. Perhaps, a visible sign of their vulnerability with each other is the fact that Gail is pregnant again. Both are scared. They both have concerns. Neither know what they will do if it happens again. But they are willing to take that risk.

Step Six questions for reflection:

1. Sit down and write five times when you have been wounded and how that has affected you today.

2. What imperfections do you hold back on sharing with others?

3. Is there any difference between what you are projecting on the outside and what is going on inside?

4. About what and with whom do you need to be more open and vulnerable today?

5. If you were to be radically honest, what kinds of weaknesses, flaws, imperfections, or failures would surface?

Forgiveness is the seventh step in this approach to spirituality. In the early years of AA, the founders picked up on the Oxford group's emphasis on forgiveness. The Oxford group had taken this central tenet directly from the scriptures. By the time that an alcoholic gets into AA, they have amassed a world of hurt and pain to themselves and all those they have come in contact with. Therefore, forgiveness is central to the program of personal recovery and spiritual growth. But what about others, those non-alcoholics, who are seeking to use this model for their growth in their spiritual life? Being able to forgive and receive forgiveness is absolutely essential if one is to progress in life in the spirit. When Gary and Gail first found out that their daughter was dead, they were absolutely stunned. The first few days after the funeral, they became very angry. Gail feared she had done something wrong for which God must be punishing her, she feared Gary blamed her, she feared that she would never ever be able to have another child. Gary projected his anger on the hospital and blamed them for not detecting a problem earlier, he blamed the doctor for not doing something to save their daughter, he blamed himself for just being angry and being such a jerk with everyone. He was angry at God for letting all the other children being born healthy, and theirs being selected to die. As much as they hated to admit it, they both blamed their daughter for not developing right and not giving them a chance to know her. Gary and Gail began to work out of their pain and sorrow as they intentionally began to forgive their doctor, the hospital, those around them, themselves and even God for letting them down and not meeting their expectations. What was harder was working through the guilt and the shame that seemed mixed in the whole situation. They found they needed to forgive each other and especially themselves. As Gary and Gail discovered the meaning of being forgiven, and what it meant to receive forgiveness, and the lengths that God went to forgive them, there was a release and new freedom to share that forgiveness with others. For them the step of forgiveness was a needed step in order for them to deal with the loss and to begin again.

Step Seven questions for reflection:

1. List who or what have you been unable to forgive and have had the hardest time forgiving.

2. What would change in or about you if you applied forgiveness to a difficult person or situation?

3. What internal or external wounds do you have that prevent you from forgiveness?

4. At the top of page 91, the verbs of AA's steps 4-11 are used. What do each of those verbs mean to you?

5. If you were to forgive yourself or another, what power would you have to give up?

AA has made famous the phrase "One day at a time." That is really practicing the eight steps of present presence. For it is the day at a time that helps people focus on time in a way that is manageable and also freeing. Being able to practice the present presence helps people do what they can and all that they can and then turn the rest over to their Higher Power. It frees people from guilt over the past and anxiety about the future. For Gary and Gail, practicing the present presence came when Gail went to the doctor for a post delivery check up. There the doctor said she saw no physical reason to prevent them from having other children. Then she asked Gail if they planned on trying to have another child. That information brought both great relief and anxiety at the same time. It was good to know that there was nothing physically or genetically wrong that had caused this. But now came the what if. What if something happens again? What if the doctor is wrong? What if there had been something they could have done differently? Both Gary and Gail knew that they could be overwhelmed by the "what if" questions. They have put their trust in God today, and trust that God will be with them and give them whatever they need to see them through whatever the future holds. As a result they did decide to have another child. Though there is no way of replacing their daughter, neither do they want that experience to prohibit them from moving into the future. They are practicing the present presence by continuing their contact with supportive friends who have lost children, by doing all that pre-natal care requires, by accepting the past, and then turning the rest over to God. It is especially this last thing of turning the rest over to God, that has helped them live one day at a time, and know that the past is okay, and that the future is assured.

Step Eight questions for reflection:

1. What issues from the past hold you from moving forward?

2. What issues create personal anxiety for the future?

3. What might change in you, in your relationships in your attitude, if you lived in complete confidence of the present presence of God?

4. What fears do you have about dying? How do they affect your living?

5. List ten ways God's presence has been made known to you today.

We are all people of control. From the earliest childhood experiences, babies are searching for what and how much they can control. It is amazing how soon a baby realizes that it can control its parents by crying. Human history could be written from the perspective of humankind's successful and not so successful attempts at controlling the environment and the people around them. Control is power and in turn power is control. Therefore, voluntarily giving up that power and control never comes easily.

What a difficult lesson it is to learn that one cannot control it all. How hard it is to accept the help, care and support from others. When trust is broken, it takes a lot of work and time to restore it. Knowing what to control and how much one can control, and then turning the rest over to God is a vital step in the spiritual road.

Gary and Gail found that their trust system was severely wrecked and damaged. They had trusted that they would have a healthy baby, they trusted the doctors to take care of any idiosyncrasies of the pregnancy, they trusted God to protect their child. When that didn't happen, their naive trust was shaken to the core. For them, restoring the trust has been an ongoing process. They have returned to this step many times. The whole issue of sorting out healthy and unhealthy dependency has been crucial for their spiritual life and growth. They review almost daily what needs to be let go of and what they need to take a hold of. They have been helped by friends and church people who have stood with them in this whole process. Their friends listened to their anger, cried with them, empathized with their pain, and also encouraged them to stand and walk again. Gary and Gail have come to the painful realization of how difficult life can be, and that they are in no way exempt from life's cruel blows. They have poured through the scriptures identifying particularly with the Psalmists who lamented over life's unfair suffering and inordinate pain, but who also discovered God's strong and abiding presence of comfort and strength to carry them through. As Gary and Gail become more secure and confident in their dependence on God's promise to be there, they have been able to let go of their grief, fear, pain, and take hold of God's love and abiding presence, and allow God to guide them into the future.

Step Nine questions for reflection:

1. How do you deal with situations and feelings of helplessness?

2. What of your needs went unmet as a child?

3. Who have you depended on that has hurt you? Helped you? What did each do?

4. What kind of things do you have a hard time letting go of?

5. What things make it hard or impossible for you to become God-dependent?

Step ten is tolerance. A man in AA told me, "Those who cannot deal with their feelings, have to deal with facts and the facts have to be perfect." Tolerance has a lot to do with people who are well on their way to truly dealing with their feelings. Dealing only with facts leads to perfectionism, and rigid self-centered definitions of rightness. When people deal with their feelings it is not "who's right," it is more a matter of "what are you feeling?" Active alcoholics can't for whatever reason deal with feelings. The AA program reconnects a person with their feelings. It is in that reconnection that there is a spiritual awakening. The more one can deal with their own

175

feelings, the more tolerant they become in dealing with the feelings of others, even when other's feelings are far different than their own.

Both Gary and Gail's parents have had a difficult time in accepting what has happened. They either refuse to talk about what happened or they diminish the importance of this still-born child. At first this hurt Gary and Gail a lot. They were looking for their parents' support and acceptance. But gradually Gary and Gail have realized that their parents are not in the same place in their own emotional and spiritual development. They asked their Pastor if children could have a greater spiritual development than their parents. Their Pastor assured them they could. Because they have worked on the steps of tolerance, no longer do Gary and Gail have to be angry, distanced and disappointed with their parents. They put less stress on themselves in trying to get their parents to change their attitudes. No longer do they have to try to get their parents to think and feel the way they do. As Gary and Gail have practiced tolerance in their own lives, they have become more gentle, kind, and calm with themselves and with each other. That tolerance has carried over to their relationship with their parents and others, in which they are far more patient and accepting. They are far more relaxed when talking and interacting on any level. As they are more tolerant, they have accepted the fact that their parents may never think or feel differently. But that is not really that important any more. To use AA language, Gary and Gail's parents had their own program to work. All they know is that tolerance has helped them grow, change, and respond in a far more spiritually centered way.

Step Ten questions for reflection:

1. Who and over what issues have you tried to convert another?

2. Reflect on your own judgmental attitudes that reflect your personal intolerance.

3. What kinds of fears prohibit you from taking the step of tolerance?

4. What deeply personal feelings of inferiority or character defects does your intolerance cover?

5. What kind of space do you need to make in yourself, in order to become more tolerant of self, others and God?

Step eleven is sharing the story. The early people in AA shared their story for the sake of their own sobriety. Christians throughout the ages have shared their personal testimony of the difference Christ has made in their lives. The spiritual journey is never complete until it takes an outward expression. "This is where I was, what happened to me, these are the things that changed me and turned my life around for me."

When Gary and Gail went through their grief they naturally turned their sorrow in on themselves. They somehow unconsciously believed and felt that they are the only ones who this kind of tragedy had happened to. No one else could know the sorrow, the disappointment, feelings of failure, despair, and depression that they felt. Then one day a woman called and identified herself and told Gail that a year earlier she too had experienced the stillbirth of a child. She knew what they must be going through. Then she told her story. That was all Gail needed. Relief was instantaneous. Somebody understood. Somebody could identify with the pain. Gail had a thousand questions, wanted to know what this woman had done. It was as if this woman was sent from heaven, a messenger from God. From that point, Gary and Gail began telling their story to others. They shared an open letter in their church newsletter. They began finding others they knew who had gone through a similar experience, but had remained silent and kept things a secret. What they found was that it was painful and hard to share their story. Neither one is a natural extrovert. But each time they told the story, there was a positive benefit and identification with those whom they were sharing with. But more importantly, there was a healing of their woundedness and a strengthening of their faith. Sharing their story was much like the story that opened this paper, where the two men lost in the forest, sit down and say, "I don't know the way out, but I can tell you what hasn't worked and maybe together we can discover some things that will." It is in the telling that the story is shared.

Step Eleven questions for reflection:

1. What are some family stories that get told and retold in your home?

2. What stories have you heard that have significantly changed you in some way?

3. Where has your story and God's story intersected?

4. How could you use a personal story to help someone struggling in some way?

It takes a great deal of spiritual and emotional maturity to move outside oneself. That is why it is the last step. All the other steps are essential and have to be in place prior to this one. For even the most benevolent and self-giving people are also self-centered. The natural tendency is to turn in on self.

This step has helped Gary and Gail use this experience to help others. Gail is working as a volunteer at the hospital, speaking to and befriending mothers who have lost children either through miscarriage or stillbirth. She and Gary are volunteering at a local chapter of Compassionate Friends, which is a support group for parents who have lost children. They have gotten to the point in their spiritual growth where they can say, "We are available. Whatever it takes, wherever God leads, we'll go." It is that availability for others that has helped them move to this step. It is their openness to God's leading that has led them to greater compassion and empathy for other's pain. It has been as they have worked on their spiritual center and established a spiritual direction that they have been able to move beyond themselves. In Christian theological language, the movement beyond oneself involves denying the self, taking up one's cross, and following Him.

Step Twelve questions for reflection:

1. What things for others do you do that really covers up your "me-centeredness?"

2. What is the difference between taking care of yourself and selfishness?

3. Having had a spiritual awakening, what message are you carrying into the world of the hurting?

4. Do you think that others can really tell the difference your spirituality has made in your life?

5. In what way(s) are you a channel of God's love and an instrument of God's peace?

These twelve steps of the spiritual journey have followed the path that people in AA have discovered. It is a sharing of what has happened to them. Because of God, their life is changed. Their spiritual approach has been tried and proven in hundreds of thousands of people, who have worked the program and found it works.

But for those of us not in AA, who are not alcoholics, it works equally well. It works because it is a scripturally faithful program based on solid biblical principles and concepts. Not only is it emotionally solid, but it is also theologically good and beneficial as well. As has been outlined in the story of Gary and Gail, one does not need to be alcoholic in order to use and profit from these twelve steps. These twelve steps can and will work, for those grieving or experiencing a loss of any kind, for those who are depressed or stressed, for those caught in dysfunctional family settings, and for those who have been abused and victimized.

The goal of spirituality is the same goal of AA and that is to become charming. We are looking to become charming not because we are already beautiful people. We are looking to find the way through the existential forest of life. For spirituality in the church to become a dominant theme and emphasis religious people are going to need to become far more spiritual in their approach to life and living. In order to do that religious people need to get serious about Big Book study. The Big Book study for Christians is the scriptures. As Christians read the scriptures reflecting on the steps that are outlined here spirituality will increase both in the individual and in the corporate body. It will make the church an attractive place to be.

The Progression and Recovery of the Alcoholic in the Disease of Alcoholism

To be read from left to right

Progression ➤

Occasional Relief Drinking

Constant Relief Drinking Commences

Urgency of First Drinks

Feelings of Guilt

Increase in Alcohol Tolerance

Memory Blackouts Increase

Onset of Memory Blackouts

Surreptitious Drinking

Drinking Bolstered with Excuses

Increasing Dependence on Alcohol

Grandiose and Aggressive Behavior

Unable to Discuss Problem

Efforts to Control Fail Repeatedly

Decrease of Ability to Stop Drinking when Others Do So

Tries Geographical Escapes

Persistent Remorse

Family and Friends Avoided

Promises and Resolutions Fail

Loss of Ordinary Will Power

Loss of Other Interests

Tremors and Early Morning Drinks

Work and Money Troubles

Decrease in Alcohol Tolerance

Onset of Lengthy Intoxications

Unreasonable Resentments

Moral Deterioration

Neglect of Food

Impaired Thinking

Physical Deterioration

Drinking with Inferiors

Indefinable Fears

Unable to Initiate Action

Obsession with Drinking

Vague Spiritual Desires

All Alibis Exhausted

Complete Defeat Admitted

Critical Phase

Chronic Phase

180

Obsessive Drinking Continues in Vicious Circles

Enlightened and Interesting Way:
Life Opens Up with Road Ahead to
Higher Levels then Ever Before.

Group Therapy and
Mutual Help Continue

Increasing Tolerance

Rationalizations Recognized

Contentment in Sobriety

Care of Personal Appearance

Confidence of Employers

First Steps Towards
Economic Stability

Appreciation of Real Values

Rebirth of Ideals

Increase of Emotional Control

New Interests Develop

Facts Faced with Courage

Adjustment to Family Needs

New Circle of Stable Friends

Desire to Escape Goes

Family and Friends
Appreciate Efforts

Return of Self-Esteem

Natural Rest and Sleep

Diminishing Fears of the
Unknown Future

Realistic Thinking

Appreciation of Possibilities
of New Way of Life

Regular Nourishment
Taken

Start of Group Therapy

Onset of New Hope

Physical Overhaul by Doctor

Spiritual Needs Examined

Right Thinking Begins

Takes Stock of Self

Meets Normal and Happy
Former Addicts

Stops Taking Alcohol

Told Addiction Can Be Arrested

Learns Alcoholism is an Illness

Honest Desire for Help

Reprinted with permission by:
Parkside Medical Service Corporation.

181

Appendix 2
Spiritual Recovery Chart

Alcoholism as a SPIRITUAL Dis-ease:

Alcohol sedates value system, which
gets indifferent, confused

Grandiosity, perfectionism, pride

Intolerance of others:
Suspicion, distrust, argues

Religion getting sick: Rigid, arrogant, unrealistic'
disenchantment with childish idea of God

Loses interest in life: "Blues"

Guilt feelings, not "at-ease" with God

Stops daily prayer, attends church out of
habit or pretense

"Nobodiness" — feels estranged, alienated, lonely

Immaturity, some irresponsibility

Life has no meaning

Anxiety, indefinable fears

Resentments: Angry at God, hostile to mention
of religion, projects fear into
concept of God as a tyrant

Moral deterioration: Dishonest, selfish

Loss of faith: Consciously rejects God,
unconsciously longs for Him — a
"sick-love" relation

Remorse: Depression, suicidal thoughts,
impaired thinking

Vague spiritual desires

Gropes for spiritual meaning

hits BOTTOM: drinks to cope
with problems of drinking

Progression and Recovery

"Weller than Well" — higher levels than
believed possible

• Unselfish: Goes out to others because
God loves them

Deeper relation to God as a loving God

Growth in proper concept of God

Prayer and meditation

Serenity, peace of soul, joy

• Increased tolerance of other

Gratitude

Appreciation of spiritual values

Rebirth of ideals

Courage, optimism — new freedom

Promptly admits when wrong

Honest: Makes amends

Return of self-esteem (God not a rescuer)

False ego deflated

Humbly asks God to remove shortcomings

Reconciliation: Personal relationship "at ease" with
God (more than just "dumping garbage")

Forgiveness: Not "why did I?" but "forgive me"
Patience: "One day at a time"
Appreciates possibility of new way of life
Trust: "Thy will be done"
• Conversion: "Let go and let God"
• Acceptance (surrender — Tiebout)
• Second BOTTOM: "Existential crisis"
Thirst for God examined ᵃhard struggle for some)
Hope dawned: Can be restored
New faith... "Came to believe"
Vague notion of Higher Power
Honest desire for help
In spiritual fog
• ADMISSION (compliance — Tiebout)

Reference List

Books:

Ackerman, Robert J. *Growing in the Shadow*. Pompano Beach: Health Communications, Inc., 1986.

_____. *Let Go And Grow*. Pompano Beach: Health Communications, Inc., 1986.

Anderson, Herbert. *The Family and Pastoral Care*. Philadelphia: Fortress Press, 1984.

Beattie, Melody. *Codependent No More*. United States of America: Hazelden Foundation, 1987.

Boisen, Anton T. *The Exploration of The Inner World*. Philadelphia: University of Pennsylvania Press, 1936.

Bradshaw, John. *Homecoming: Championing Your Inner Child*. New York: Bantam Books, 1990.

Bundesen, Lynne. *God Dependency*. New York: Crossroad, 1989.

Fowler, James W. *Stages of Faith*. San Francisco: Harper and Row, 1981.

Friel, John and Linda. *Adult Children, The Secrets of Dysfunctional Families*. Deerfield Beach: Health Communications, 1988.

Grollman, Earl A. *Explaining Death to Children*. Boston: Beacon Press, 1967.

James, William. *The Varieties of Religious Experiences*. New York: Signet, 1958.

Jordan, Merle R. *Taking on the Gods*. Nashville: Abingdon, 1986.

Keller, John E. *Let Go, Let God*. Minneapolis: Augsburg Publishing House, 1985.

Kurtz, Ernest. *Not-God, A History of Alcoholics Anonymous*. Center City: Hazelden Foundation, 1979.

Kushner, Harold. *When Bad Things Happen to Good People*. New York: Schocken Books, 1981.

——————— . *Who Needs God*. New York: Summit Books, 1989.

Miller, Alice. *For Your Own Good*. New York: Farrar Straus, Giroux, 1983.

Minuchin, Salvador. *Families & Family Therapy*. Cambridge, Massachusetts: Harvard University Press, 1974.

Morreim, Dennis C. *The Road To Recovery*. Minneapolis: Augsburg, 1990.

Neill, John R. and Kniskern, David P. *From Psyche To System, The Evolving Therapy of Carl Whitaker*. New York: The Guilford Press, 1982.

Nouwen, Henri J. M. *Intimacy*. San Francisco: Harper and Row, 1969.

Patton, John. *Is Human Forgiveness Possible?* Nashville: Abingdon Press, 1985.

Peck, M. Scott. *The Different Drum*. New York: Simon and Schuster, 1987.

——————— . *People of the Lie*. New York: Simon and Schuster, 1983.

——————— . *The Road Less Traveled*. New York: Simon and Schuster, 1978.

Powell, John. *Happiness Is An Inside Job*. Valencia, California: Tabor Publishing, 1989.

_____. *Why Am I Afraid To Tell You Who I Am?* Valencia, California: Tabor Publishing, 1969.

Schaef, Anne Wilson. *Co-Dependence Misunderstood — Mistreated*. San Francisco: Harper and Row Publishers, 1986.

Simon, Dr. Sidney B. and Suzanne. *Forgiveness*. New York: Warner Books, 1990.

Smedes, Lewis B. *Caring & Commitment*. San Francisco: Harper and Row, 1988.

_____. *Forgive & Forget*. San Francisco: Harper and Row, 1984.

Tiebout, Harry M. *Alcoholism — Its Nature and Treatment*. New York: The National Council On Alcoholism, Inc., 1958.

_____. *The Act of Surrender In The Therapeutic Process*. New York: The National Council On Alcoholism, Inc., 1945.

_____. *Conversion As A Psychological Phenomenon*. New York: The National Council On Alcoholism, Inc., 1944.

_____. *Ego Factors In Surrender*. New York: The National Council On Alcoholism, Inc., 1954.

_____. *Intervention In Psychotherapy*. New York: The National Council On Alcoholism, Inc., 1964.

_____. *The Role Of Psychiatry In The Field Of Alcoholism*. New York: The National Council On Alcoholism, Inc., 1951.

Whitaker, Carl A. and Bumberry, William M. *Dancing With The Family*. New York: Brunner/Mazel, 1988.

_____. *Midnight Musings of a Family Therapist*. New York: W. W. Norton & Company, 1989.

Woititz, Janet G. *Struggle For Intimacy*. Deerfield Beach, Fla: Health Communications, Inc., 1985.

Endnotes

Chapter 1
Beginning The Spiritual Journey

[1]M. Scott Peck, *The Road Less Traveled* (New York: Simon and Schuster, 1978), 15.

Chapter 2
The Search Begins

[1]Ernest Kurtz, *Not-God, A History of Alcohlics Anonymous* (Center City: The Hazelden Foundation, 1979), 15.

[2]James W. Fowler, *Stages of Faith* (San Francisco: Harper and Row, 1981), 5.

[3]Merle R. Jordon, *Taking On The Gods* (Nashville: Abingdon, 1986), 29.

[4]Ibid., 22.

[5]Ibid., 24.

[6]Kurtz, 21.

Chapter 3
Step One — Crisis

[1]Harold Kushner, *When Bad Things Happen to Good People* (New York: Schocken Books, 1981).

[2]Kurtz, 61.

[3]M. Scott Peck, *People Of The Lie* (New York: Simon and Schuster, 1983).

[4]William James, *The Varieties Of Religious Experience* (New York: The New American Library, Inc., 1958).

[5]Kurtz, 21.

[6]Anton T. Boisen, *The Exploration of The Inner World* (Philadelphia: University of Pennsylvania Press, 1936).

Chapter 4
Step Two — Surrender

[1]Harry M. Tiebout, *The Act of Surrender In The Therapeutic Process* (New York: The National Council On Alcoholism, Inc., 1945), 6.

[2]Ibid.

[3]Robert J. Ackerman, *Growing In The Shadow* (Pompano Beach: Health Communications, Inc., 1986), 4ff.

[4]John and Linda Friel, *Adult Children, The Secrets of Dysfunctional Families* (Deerfield Beach: Health Communications, 1988), 24.

[5]Ibid., 108.

[6]Kurtz, 245.

[7]Harry M. Tiebout, *Ego Factors In Surrender* (New York: The National Council On Alcoholism, Inc., 1954), 612.

[8]Lewis B. Smedes, *Caring & Commitment* (San Francisco: Harper and Row, 1988), 10.

[9]Ibid., 29.

[10]Tiebout, 9-10.

[11]M. Scott Peck, *People Of The Lie* (New York: Simon and Schuster, 1983), 83.

[12]Kurtz, 184.

[13]Peck, 43.

[14]Ibid.

[15]Ibid., 162.

[16]Tiebout, 618.

[17]Anne Wilson Schaef, *Co-Dependence Misunderstood — Mistreated* (San Francisco: Harper and Row Publishers, 1986), 85.

[18]Ackerman, 48-84.

[19]Tiebout, 620.

[20]Kurtz, 182.

[21]John E. Keller, *Let Go, Let God* (Minneapolis: Augsburg Publishing House, 1985), 46.

Chapter 5
Step Three — Conversion

[1]Harry M. Tiebout, *Conversion As A Psychological Phenomenon* (New York: The National Council On Alcoholism, Inc., 1944), 2.

[2]Ibid., 11.

[3]Kurtz, 9.

[4]Ibid., 34.

[5]Tiebout, 2-3.

[6]Harry M. Tiebout, *Alcoholism — Its Nature and Treatment* (New York: The National Council On Alcoholism, Inc., 1958), 10.

[7]Peck, 37.

Chapter 6
Step Four — Emptiness

[1]M. Scott Peck, *The Different Drum* (New York: Simon and Schuster, 1987), 217.

[2]Ibid., 212.

[3]Ibid., 222-223.

Chapter 7
Step Five — Centering

[1]Melody Beattie, *Codependent No More* (USA: Hazelden Foundation, 1987), 211.

Chapter 8
Step Six — Vulnerability

[1]Alice Miller, *For Your Own Good* (New York: Farrar, Straus, Giroux, 1983).

[2]Alice Miller, *Thou Shalt Not Be Aware* (New York: Farrar, Straus, Siroux, 1981).

[3]John Bradshaw, *Homecoming: Championing Your Inner Child* (New York: Bantam Books, 1990).

[4]Peck, 231.

[5]Ibid., 226-227.

[6]Ibid., 231.

[7]Kurtz, 197.

[8]Ibid., 198.

[9]John Powell, *Why Am I Afraid To Tell You Who I Am?* (Valencia, California: Tabor Publishing, 1969).

[10]Kurtz, 197.

[11]Carl Whitaker, *Midnight Musings of a Family Therapist* (New York: W. W. Norton and Co., 1989), 196.

Chapter 9
Step Seven — Forgiveness

[1]Alice Miller, *For Your Own Good*, 248.

[2]Robert J. Ackerman, *Let Go And Grow* (Pompano Beach: Health Communications, Inc., 1986), 139.

[3]Carl A. Whitaker, 50.

[4]John Patton, *Is Human Forgiveness Possible?* (Nashville: Abingdon Press, 1985), 37.

[5]Smedes, 152.

[6]Miller, 248.

[7]Patton.

[8]Lewis B. Smedes, *Forgive & Forget* (San Francisco: Harper and Row, 1984).

[9]Dr. Sidney B. and Suzanne Simon, *Forgiveness* (New York: Warner Books, 1990).

[10]Smedes, xii.

[11]Patton, 93.

[12]Ibid., 153.

[13]Ibid., 174.

[14]Ibid., 161.

[15]Smedes, 151.

Chapter 10
Step Eight — Present Presence

[1]Whitaker, 200.

[2]Ibid., 52.

[3]Ibid., 53.

[4]Ackerman, *Growing In The Shadow*, 116.

[5]Earl A. Grollman, *Explaining Death To Children* (Boston: Beacon Press, 1967), 240-241.

[6]Ibid., 239.

[7]Whitaker, 54.

[8]Kushner, 203.

[9]Ibid.

[10]Ibid., 203.

Chapter 11
Step Nine — Restoring a Healthy Dependence

[1]Beattie, 46.

[2]Friel, 33.

[3]Ibid., 157.

[4]Friel, 81-90.

[5]Salvador, Minuchin, *Families And Family Therapy* (Cambridge: Harvard University Press, 1974), 54-56.

[6]Herbert, Anderson, *The Family and Pastoral Care* (Philadelphia: Fortress Press, 1984), 12.

[7]Friel, 59.

[8]Schaef, 35.

[9]Ibid., 37.

[10]Anderson, 13.

[11]Schaef, 21.

[12]Ibid., 29.

[13]Ackerman, 114.

[14]Friel, 28.

[15]Ibid., 71.

[16]Lynne Bundesen, *God Dependency* (New York: Crossroad, 1989), 65.

[17]Miller, 65.

[18]Ibid., 73.

[19]Ibid., 106.

[20]Kurtz, 209.

[21]Bundeson, 23.

[22]Ibid., 28.

[23]Kurtz, 209.

[24]Bundeson, 37.

[25]Ibid., 58.

[26]Kurtz, 125.

[27]Beattie, 121.

[28]Bundeson, 76.

[29]Ibid., preface.

[30]Ibid., iv.

Chapter 12
Step Ten — Tolerance

[1]Tiebout, *Conversion As A Psychological Phenonmenon.*

Chapter 13
Step Eleven — Sharing the Story

[1]Kurtz, 93.

[2]Ibid., 191.

Chapter 14
Step Twelve — Movement Beyond the Self

[1]Whitaker, 49.

[2]Ackerman, 94.

[3]Kurtz, 35.

[4]Kushner, 203.

[5]Ibid., 204.

[6]John Powell, *Happiness Is An Inside Job* (Valencia, California: Tabor Publishing, 1989), 76.